THE GLOBAL FOOL

A History of the Clown
by Thomas Buchheister
Creative Spark Publishing

© 2025 Thomas Buchheister
All rights reserved.
No part of this publication may be reproduced, stored in a retrieval system, or transmitted in any form or by any means—electronic, mechanical, photocopying, recording, or otherwise—without the prior written permission of the publisher, except for brief quotations used in critical reviews or scholarly work.

This book is a work of nonfiction. Every reasonable effort has been made to ensure the accuracy of information and sourcing. Opinions expressed are those of the author.

Published by Creative Spark Publishing
Printed in the United States of America

ISBN: 9798288543890
First Edition

Cover design and interior illustrations by the author and AI-enhanced engraving techniques.
Disclaimer:
This book is intended for educational and scholarly purposes. All referenced materials and cultural depictions are presented with respect and a focus on historical context. Interpretations of clown traditions may vary by region and practitioner.

Thank You

Thank you for joining me on this exploration through the tangled history, joy, fear, and symbolism of the clown.

This book was written with deep appreciation for performers past and present who step into absurdity to reveal something true.

If this work made you laugh, reflect, or see differently—I'd be honored if you shared it with others or left a review.

— Thomas Buchheister

This book is proudly published by a Disabled Veteran Owned Business.

The Global Fool: A History of the Clown

Preface

Ask two people what they think of when they hear the word "clown," and you are likely to get two wildly different answers. One will picture the gentle, bumbling host of a children's TV show. The other will imagine a sinister figure lurking in the shadows of a horror film. How did a single character come to embody both our fondest childhood memories and our deepest fears?

This paradox is the starting point for our story. The modern clown lives a double life as both a benevolent healer and a malevolent monster and understanding how we arrived at this point is to understand the entire, epic history of the fool. This book is a deep dive into that history, an investigation into how a sacred ritualist became a circus superstar, and how that superstar became a cultural bogeyman. It is the story of a painted smile and the many, often contradictory, meanings we have projected onto it for millennia. To understand the clown is to understand our own shifting relationship with innocence, chaos, laughter, and fear.

CHAPTER ONE

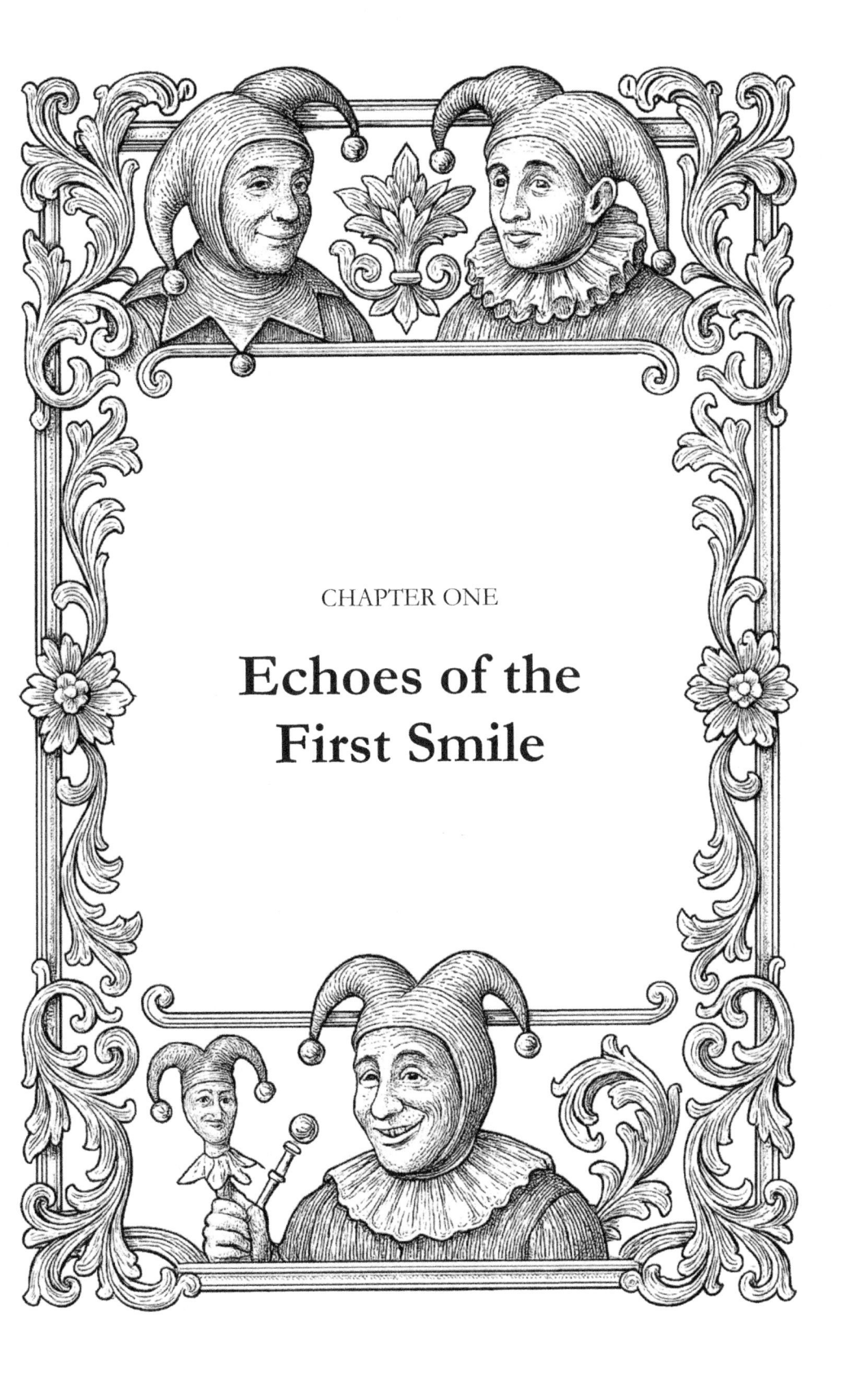

Echoes of the First Smile

Before the red nose, the oversized shoes, and the rainbow wig, there was the fool. Before the slapstick, the squirting flower, and the tiny car, there was the jester. The history of the clown is not merely a chronicle of circus acts and children's parties; it is a profound journey into the very heart of human society, a reflection of our need for laughter, truth, and a healthy dose of chaos. The painted face we recognize today is the modern mask of an ancient archetype, a figure who has danced on the fringes of power, whispered truth to kings, and held a mirror to our own follies for millennia. This is not just the story of an entertainer, but the biography of an essential human character who, in his many guises, has served as a ritualistic shaman, a social critic, and a potent symbol of our shared, imperfect humanity. From the sacred courts of pharaohs to the raucous stages of Renaissance Italy, and from the gaslit theaters of London to the three-ring circuses of America, the clown's journey is a twisting, surprising, and often poignant tale that reveals as much about us as it does about the character himself.

The Sacred Fool: Ancient Origins

The earliest whispers of the clown can be traced back not to a stage, but to the altar and the throne. In the nascent civilizations of the ancient world, the figure we might retroactively label a clown was rarely a simple entertainer. Instead, they were often sacred fools, individuals whose physical peculiarities or mental eccentricities set them apart, granting them a unique and often protected status. Their role was a complex amalgam of priest, shaman, and social commentator. It was believed that their perceived "otherness" gave them a unique connection to the divine, allowing them to speak honesty forbidden to ordinary men and women.

In Ancient Egypt, as early as the Fifth Dynasty (circa 2400 BCE), records depict the *Danga*, a pygmy from Central Africa, serving in the court of the pharaoh. Valued for their diminutive stature and their skill as dancers, the Danga performed ritualistic dances intended to please the gods and bring joy to the earthly ruler. While their function was entertainment, it was entertainment steeped in religious significance. They were not merely amusing; they were a living conduit to a primordial, spiritual world, their performances in the form of divine placation. Their physical difference was not a source of ridicule but a mark of their special, sacred purpose. They were fools in the sense that they operated outside the rigid social norms of the court, but their folly was holy.

This concept of the sacred fool echoed across the Mediterranean in Ancient Greece. While Greek theatre would later give birth to more formalized comic characters, the seeds were sown in figures who used humor and absurdity to provoke thought. The character of the *bomolochos*, or buffoon, in Old Comedy was a stock figure known for his vulgarity, gluttony, and witty absurdity. He was often a foil to the *eirôn*, the clever, self-deprecating protagonist. Even the philosopher Socrates was accused by his contemporaries of playing the part of a sophisticated fool, using irony and feigned ignorance to expose the pretensions of Athens' most powerful citizens. His method of questioning, of playing the simpleton to reveal a deeper truth, is a foundational element of the clown's eventual intellectual toolkit.

The Romans, in turn, inherited and adapted these traditions. Their society featured a menagerie of comic performers, from the street mimes to the stock characters of Atellan Farce, a form of rustic, improvised comedy. One of the most significant of these was the *Sannio*, a mime who was famous for his ability to pull grotesque faces and engage in slapstick with his fellow actors. The Sannio was a purely comic figure, a target of physical humor, but another figure, the *stupidus* (from which we derive our word "stupid"), played the role of the bald-headed fool or blockhead. Often wearing a pointed hat and a multi-colored patchwork garment—an early ancestor of the jester's motley—the stupidus was the butt of jokes and pranks. Yet, even here, a certain license was granted. His foolishness was his shield, allowing him to absorb the comic blows that maintained social order and provided a release valve for the audience. These Roman clowns, though more secular than their Egyptian counterparts, still operated within a defined social function: to be the vessel for mockery, and in doing so, to entertain and instruct.

Perhaps the most potent example of the sacred fool archetype is found far from Europe, in the traditions of Native American cultures. Across numerous tribes, the "Contrary" or "Sacred Clown" was a highly respected and spiritually significant figure. These individuals were bound by a sacred duty to live their lives in reverse, saying "yes" when they meant "no," shivering in the summer heat, and walking backward. Their bizarre and often disruptive behavior served a crucial social and religious purpose. By acting in opposition to all accepted norms, they forced their community to question the nature of those norms. They were a living, breathing paradox, demonstrating the limitations of human rules and reminding people of a larger, more chaotic spiritual reality. During sacred ceremonies, they would often mock the proceedings, burlesque the most solemn rituals, and treat the holiest objects with comical irreverence. This was not sacrilege; it was a form of profound spiritual honesty, a way of ensuring that religious practice did not become stale, rigid, or self-important. The Sacred Clown kept the spiritual world vibrant and alive by injecting it with the unexpected, the absurd, and the hilarious. They were the ultimate tricksters, and their antics were a powerful medicine against the dangers of dogma and conformity.

TIMELINE OF THE CLOWN

2400 BCE	200 BCE	1100 CE	1900S
Sacred pygmy dancers at Egyptian court	Roman Sannio (mime roles)	Court jesters in medieval Europe	Silent film clowns (Chaplin, Keaton)

1100 C	1500s	1970s
Court jesters in medieval Europe	Rise of *Commedia dell'arte*	Patch Adams and therapeutic clowning

From Court Jester to Italian Stage: The Medieval and Renaissance Clown

As the Roman Empire crumbled and Europe entered the Middle Ages, the clown archetype found a new and enduring home in the halls of power. The sacred fool of antiquity evolved into the court jester, a figure whose proximity to kings and nobles granted him a unique and precarious position. The jester, or fool, was a fixture in nearly every royal court, from the grandest empires to the most modest feudal manors. Dressed in his iconic motley, cap, and bells, he was a living symbol of mirth and a stark counterpoint to the rigid decorum of courtly life.

The role of the court jester was paradoxical. On one hand, he was a domestic servant, a plaything for the monarch, expected to entertain on demand with a mix of acrobatics, music, juggling, and witty banter. He was often the only person at court who could speak truth to power without fear of execution. His official status as a "fool" afforded him a license for candor that was denied to the most powerful dukes and advisors. Shielded by his motley, he could criticize a king's foolish policies, mock the vanity of a queen, or expose the corruption of a bishop through a clever riddle, a satirical song, or a well-timed joke. The bells on his cap, which seemed to signal his foolishness, were in fact a warning: the truth was coming, wrapped in the guise of humor. Figures like Triboulet, the jester to King Louis XII and Francis I of France, became legendary for their sharp wit and daring impudence. When a nobleman threatened to beat him to death for an insulting remark, Triboulet appealed to the king, who offered to have the nobleman executed. The jester cleverly replied, "I would prefer, Your Majesty, if you would have him beaten to death a day before he does it to me." This blend of wit and mock stupidity was the jester's stock-in-trade.

However, this protected status was always fragile. The Jester had to be a master of social dynamics, able to read the monarch's mood with perfect accuracy. A joke that might earn a laugh one day could earn a flogging the next. This constant dance on the edge of a razor gave the court jester a tragic dimension, a theme William Shakespeare would later explore with profound insight. In plays like *King Lear*, the Fool is not merely comic relief but the voice of reason and loyalty, his nonsensical rhymes and sad songs revealing a wisdom that the mad king can no longer grasp. The Shakespearian fool represents the pinnacle of the archetype, a character who is both the funniest and the wisest person on stage.

While jesters were holding court in the castles of the north, a theatrical revolution was brewing under the Italian sun. The Renaissance saw the birth of *Commedia dell'arte*, a form of popular, improvised theatre that would permanently shape the future of clowning. Troupes of professional actors traveled from town to town, performing on makeshift stages in public squares. They relied not on written scripts, but on stock scenarios (*scenari*) and a cast of well-defined stock characters, each with a distinctive mask, costume, and set of physical behaviors, or *lazzi*.

Within this framework, the clown was splintered into a fascinating array of types, primarily the *Zanni*. The Zanni were the servant characters, the comic engines of the plot. They were perpetually hungry, driven by the most basic desires, and their schemes to get food, money, or a moment's rest almost always ended in disaster. There were typically two Zanni in a performance: one clever and scheming, the other foolish and bumbling. The most famous and influential of these was Arlecchino, or Harlequin. With his patchwork costume (a stylized representation of a poor servant's mended clothes) and black mask, Harlequin was an astonishingly agile and amoral trickster. He was a master acrobat, constantly in motion, driven by his appetites but possessed of a cunning cat-like wit. His primary prop was the *batocio*, or slapstick—a wooden paddle with a hinged flap that created a loud "smacking" sound when it hit another actor, allowing for the illusion of comic violence without causing actual harm. The term "slapstick comedy" is a direct legacy of this simple but effective prop.

Contrasting with Harlequin was the character of Pierrot (or Pedrolino). Originally one of the Zanni, Pierrot evolved into a more distinct and melancholier figure. Dressed in a loose-fitting white tunic with large buttons, his face was often powdered white, making him the first recognizable "whiteface" clown. Unlike the mischievous Harlequin, Pierrot was the sad clown, the eternal romantic optimist doomed to have his heart broken. He was trusting, naive, and hopelessly in love with the flirtatious Columbina, who almost always chose Harlequin over him. His comedy was born of pathos, of his earnest failures and unrequited love. This character, with his silent longing and tear-streaked face, introduced a crucial element to the clowning tradition: the idea that the funniest performances are often tinged with a deep and relatable sadness. The silent, mournful Pierrot would become a powerful artistic symbol, influencing everyone from pantomime artists to modernist painters for centuries to come.

A HISTORY OF THE CLOWN

CLASSICAL ANTIQUITY — MEDIEVAL ERA — PIERROT — 1900

JESTER   PIERROT   AUGUSTE CLOWN

Grimaldi and the Rise of the Modern Circus Clown

As the 18th century gave way to the 19th century, the traditions of the court jester and the Commedia dell'arte archetypes began to merge and transform, catalyzed by the Industrial Revolution and the rise of new forms of popular entertainment. The formal court jester had largely faded into history, but the spirit of the clown found a new, vibrant stage in the raucous, gaslit world of the English pantomime and, most importantly, the nascent circus. It was in this environment that one man, more than any other, would synthesize the disparate elements of clowning's past and create the template for the modern clown: Joseph Grimaldi.

Born in 1778 into a family of dancers and comedians, Grimaldi was a creature of the London stage. He made his debut as a toddler and grew to become the undisputed king of pantomime, a uniquely British form of musical comedy theatre. Pantomime stories were loosely based on fairy tales or Commedia dell'arte scenarios, but their main appeal lay in spectacular stage effects, musical numbers, and the comic performances of their leading clown. Grimaldi elevated this role into an art form. He was not just a player in the story; he was the star, the anarchic force of nature around whom the entire production revolved.

His clown character, affectionately known as "Joey," was a revolutionary creation. Grimaldi shed the traditional patchwork costume of Harlequin and the loose white garments of Pierrot. Instead, he designed his own look: a garish, brightly colored costume, often adorned with pom-poms and frills, with his face and neck painted a stark, ghostly white. Upon this base, he added large, expressive red triangles on his cheeks, thick black eyebrows that arched into the heavens, and a wild blue crest of hair. It was a mask of pure paint, designed to be seen from the back rows of the enormous Drury Lane and Covent Garden theatres. This was the birth of the modern clown face.

But Grimaldi's genius was not just in his makeup. He was a

master of physical comedy, a brilliant satirist, and an expert at engaging directly with his audience. His performances were a whirlwind of slapstick, tumbling, and comic pratfalls, but they were also filled with topical jokes, political satire, and catchy songs. He perfected the art of the "catchphrase," and his famous song, "Hot Codlins," about a gin-selling gingerbread man, became an anthem for London audiences who would sing along with gusto. He was at once a mischievous rogue, a bumbling innocent, and a sharp social critic. He took the agility of Harlequin and the pathos of Pierrot and combined them with the topical wit of the court jester, creating a character who was entirely new and yet deeply familiar. He was so influential that to this day, clowns are often referred to as "Joeys" in his honor.

Grimaldi's reign, however, was tragically short. The brutal physicality of his performance took a devastating toll on his body. He was plagued by chronic pain and respiratory illness, and was forced into an early retirement, a broken man. His farewell speech to the London audience was a moment of profound public sorrow, revealing the deep connection he had forged with his public. His life story, a mix of public adulation and private suffering, cemented the trope of the "sad clown" in the popular imagination, the idea of the man who makes the world laugh while secretly weeping inside.

As Grimaldi was defining the theatrical clown, a new arena was being born that would become the clown's most iconic home: the circus. Philip Astley, a former cavalryman, is credited with creating the modern circus in London in 1768. He discovered that a 42-foot diameter ring was the ideal size for performing equestrian tricks, as centrifugal force helped him keep his balance on a cantering horse. To break up the equestrian acts, he hired acrobats, jugglers, and, crucially, a clown. The first circus clowns were essentially comic riding masters who would burlesque the more serious equestrian acts, pretending to be unable to stay on their horse. This "clown on a horse" was one of the earliest staples of the circus.

With the introduction of the large canvas tent in the 1820s, the circus became a mobile spectacle, able to travel across Europe and, most importantly, America. It was in the expansive one-ring, and later three-ring, circuses of the United States that the clown character would diversify and flourish into the types we recognize today. The legacy of Grimaldi's "Joey" was adapted for this new, larger environment. The circus clown couldn't rely on subtle wordplay or topical satire that might be lost in a noisy tent. Their comedy had to be bigger, broader, and more physical. The circus became the laboratory where the modern clown character was refined and perfected, setting the stage for the American archetypes who would soon dominate the 20th century.

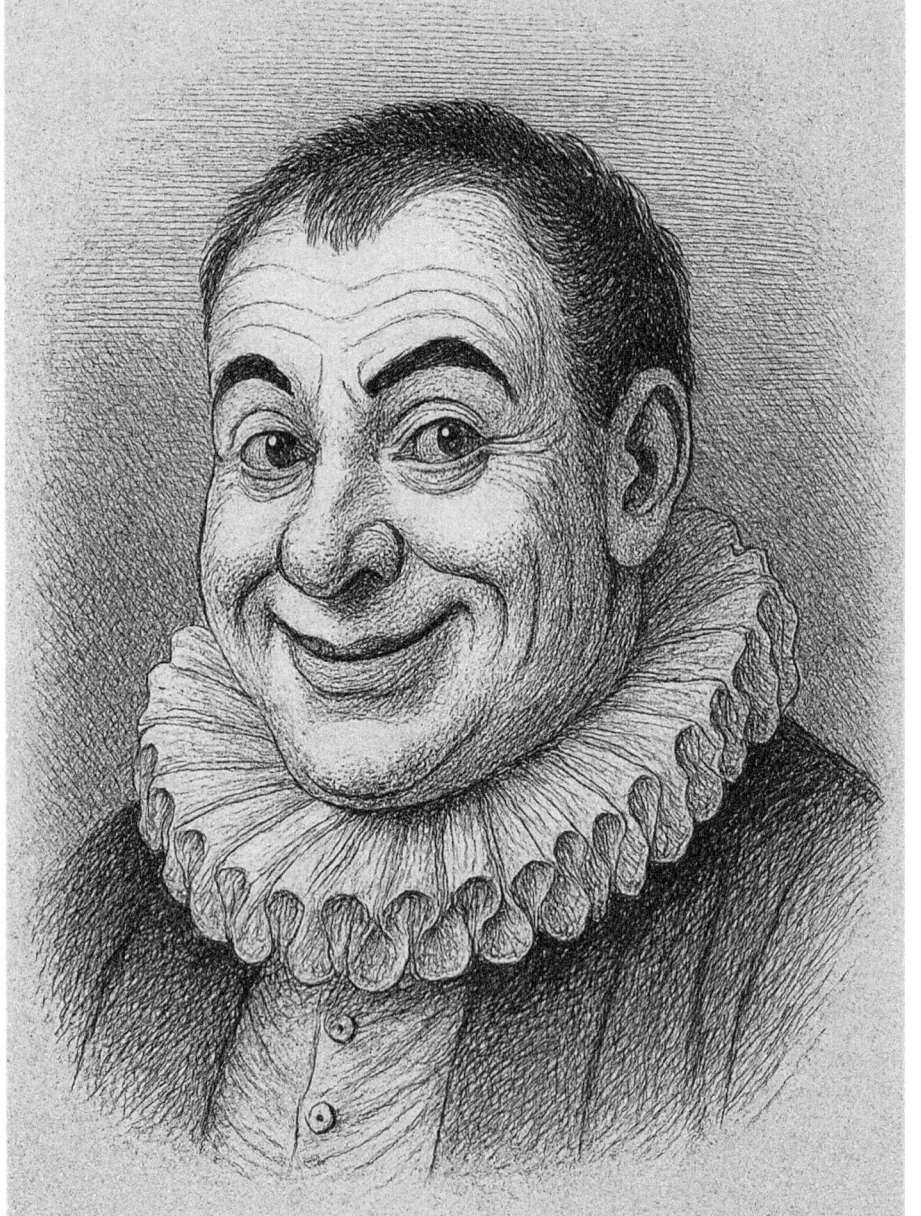

JOSEPH GRIMALDI
AS "JOEY"

CHAPTER TWO

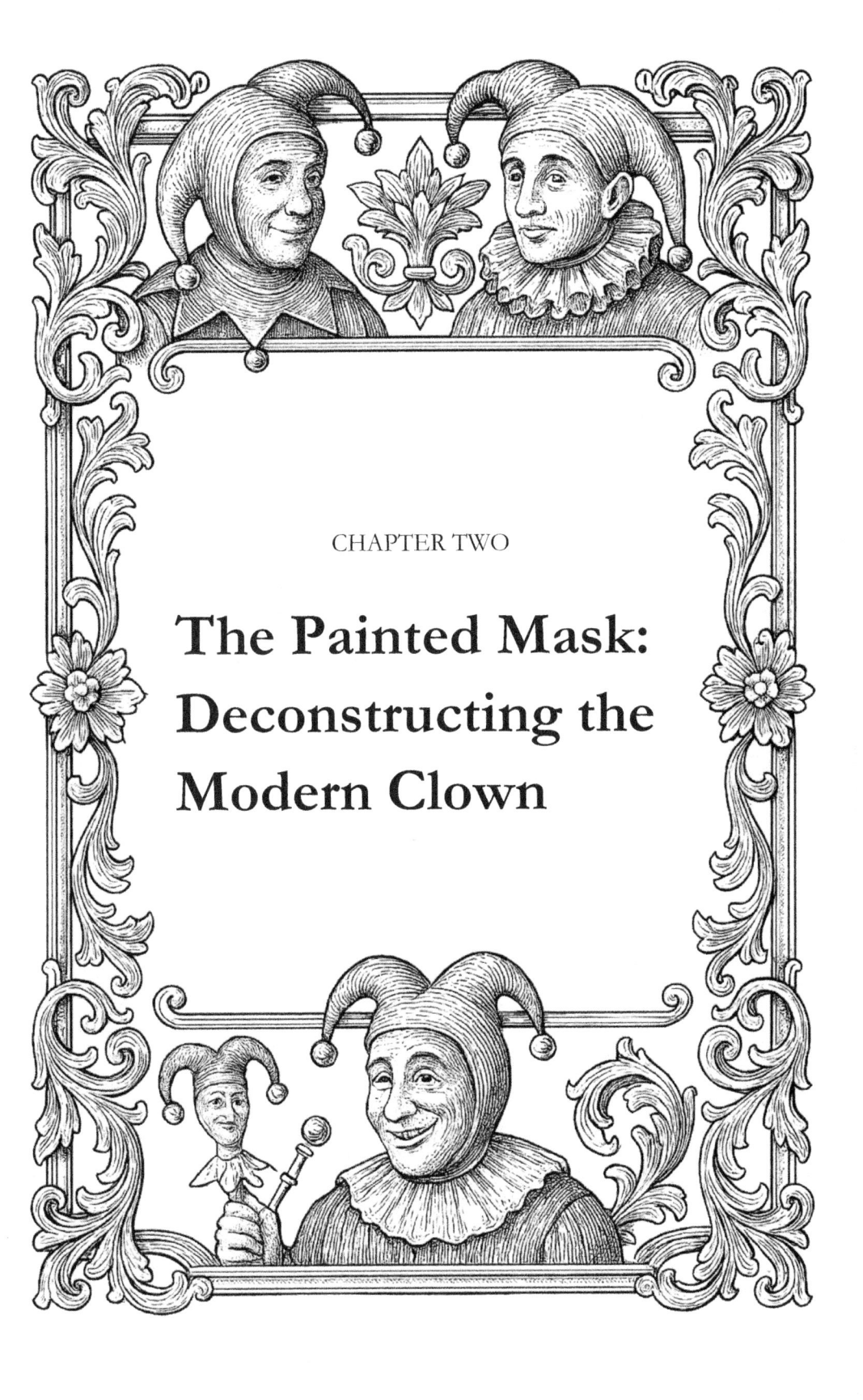

The Painted Mask: Deconstructing the Modern Clown

The journeys of the clown did not end with the dimming of the circus spotlight or the flicker of the first television sets. As the 20th century progressed, the clown archetype, having been forged in the crucible of the American circus, fractured and evolved once more. It leaped from the sawdust ring onto the silver screen, found a new intellectual home in the avant-garde theatres of Europe, and burrowed deep into the collective psyche, where its painted smile began to evoke not only laughter but a profound and unsettling fear. The modern clown became less of a single character and more of a complex spectrum of possibilities. It was an art form to be studied, a psychological symbol to be analyzed, and a cinematic trope to be endlessly reinvented. The story of the modern clown is the story of how the ancient fool learned to navigate the complexities of a new world, a world of mass media, psychoanalysis, and global interconnectedness. It is the tale of how the painted mask became both a tool for profound artistic expression and a mirror reflecting our most deep-seated anxieties.

The Performer's Art: Beyond the Big Top

While the American circus was perfecting its iconic archetypes, a quieter and more intellectual revolution in clowning was taking shape across the Atlantic. In the mid-20th century, a new generation of European theatre practitioners began to look beyond the gags and routines of the circus clown, seeking to understand and teach clowning not as a set of tricks, but as a fundamental state of being and a profound theatrical art form. This movement shifted the clown's home from the circus tent to the experimental "black box" theatre, transforming it from a stock character into a deeply personal and vulnerable creation.

The most influential figure in this transformation was Jacques Lecoq. At his legendary Parisian school, L'École Internationale de Théâtre Jacques Lecoq, founded in 1956, he developed a pedagogy that would influence generations of actors, directors, and clowns. Lecoq was not interested in teaching students how to *act* like a clown; he was interested in helping them *find* their own inner clown. His method was centered on physical awareness, improvisation, and the concept of the "neutral mask." Students first had to master neutrality, stripping away their personal habits and psychological tensions to become a blank slate. Only from this state of perfect calm and availability could the true character emerge.

Lecoq's training for clowns was famously rigorous. He would encourage students to discover their personal "flops" or vulnerability and to build a character around it. The goal was to find the state of sublime stupidity and openness where the performer is completely present and responsive to the audience. He famously used the "red nose," the smallest mask in the world, not as a costume piece but as a tool for discovery. Once a student put on the red nose, they were expected to enter a state of heightened playfulness and idiocy. Lecoq taught that the clown exists in a state of constant failure but celebrates that failure with an indomitable spirit. This approach, often called the "via negativa," was about finding the clown by removing the layers of social conditioning and intellectual pretense. The result was not a generic Whiteface or Auguste, but a unique clown persona born from the actor's own body, personality, and vulnerabilities.

Another towering figure in this theatrical clowning movement was Philippe Gaulier, a former student and teacher at Lecoq's school who went on to found his own influential institution. Gaulier's approach was more provocative and confrontational. He sought to find the clown through "le jeu," or "the game," and the pleasure of being on stage. He was notorious for his brutal honesty, often shouting "Boring!" at his students until they abandoned their preconceived ideas and found a genuine sense of play and connection with the audience. For Gaulier, the clown is a beautiful idiot who finds immense pleasure in their own stupidity and in the complicity of the audience's laughter. While Lecoq's method was more poetic and analytical, Gaulier's was a baptism by fire, forcing the performer to find a state of uninhibited joy and mischief.

Together, these and other European masters of "theatre clown" established a new philosophy. They divorced the clown from the circus narrative and re-established it as a powerful tool for the actor and a unique genre of theatre. This art form emphasizes the shared vulnerability between the performer and the audience. The theatrical clown does not hide behind a character; they reveal their most ridiculous, pathetic, and beautiful self. They are not just funny; they are a moving testament to the resilience of the human spirit in the face of its own magnificent incompetence. This movement created a new lineage of performers, like Slava Polunin with his ethereal *Snowshow* and the duo behind the British troupe Complicité, who used the principles of clowning to create deeply moving and visually stunning works of theatre, proving that the red nose could be a key to unlocking not just laughter, but profound artistic truth.

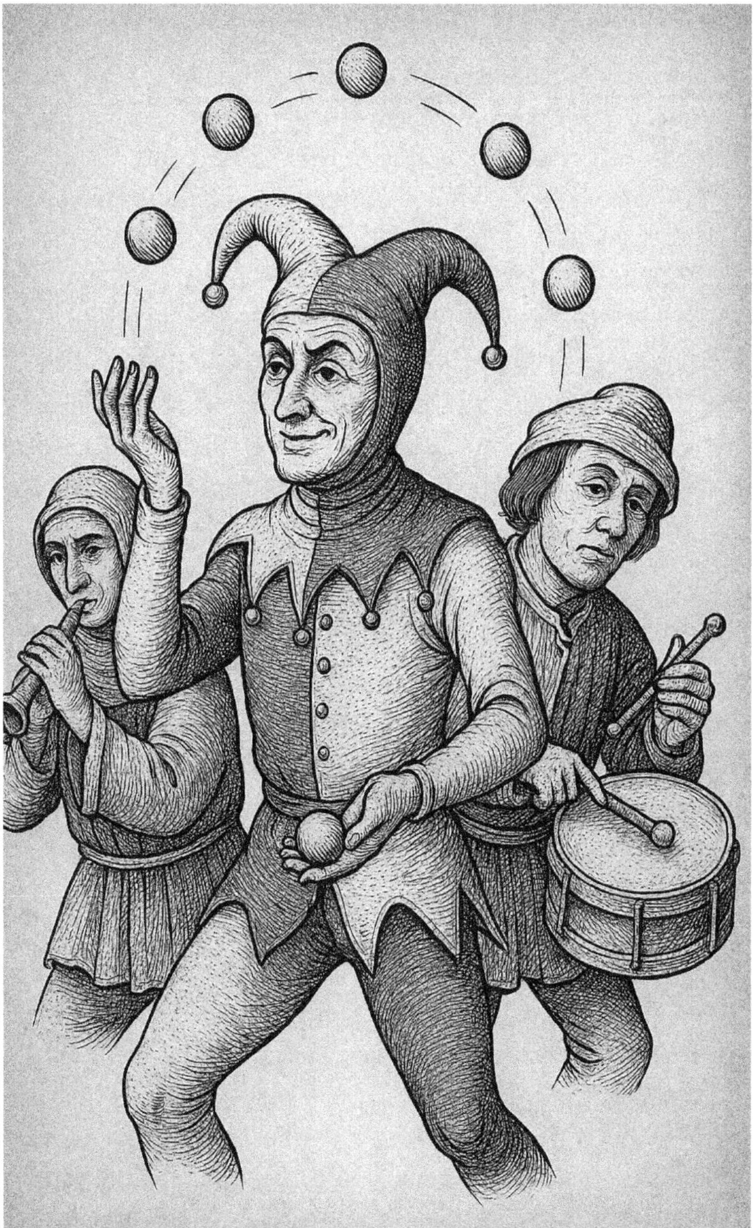

The Celluloid Clown: Laughter in Black and White

As the art of clowning was being deconstructed in European theatres, it was exploding into a global phenomenon through the new and powerful medium of cinema. The early 20th century was the era of the silent film, and with no dialogue to rely on, comedy had to be purely physical. This created the perfect conditions for a new kind of clown to emerge, one whose performance was a ballet of slapsticks, mime, and subtle emotional expression captured in the intimate close-up. The silent film comedians were not just actors playing a part; they were direct descendants of the Zanni, the jesters, and the circus clowns, adapting the ancient craft for a revolutionary new stage.

The undisputed king of this new domain was Charlie Chaplin. His iconic character, "The Tramp," was a global evolution of the American hobo clown archetype, but Chaplin infused him with a pathos and social commentary that resonated with millions. With his ill-fitting suit, bowler hat, bamboo cane, and trademark waddle, the Tramp was the ultimate outsider, the underdog navigating a harsh and unforgiving modern world. Chaplin was a master of blending hilarious slapstick with moments of heartbreaking sentimentality. In *The Gold Rush* (1925), his starving Tramp character performs the "Oceana Roll," a delicate and delightful dance using two forks and bread rolls, a moment of pure creative joy in the face of desperation. In *City Lights* (1931), the final scene, in which a formerly blind flower girl recognizes the Tramp as her anonymous benefactor, is one of the most poignant moments in film history. The Tramp's face, caught between hope and fear, communicates a depth of emotion that words could never capture. Chaplin proved that the clown could not only make audiences laugh, but could make them weep, often in the same breath.

If Chaplin was the sentimental heart of silent comedy, Buster Keaton was its stoic, acrobatic soul. Known as "The Great Stone Face" for his unwavering, deadpan expression, Keaton's comedy came from the contrast between his passive demeanor and the breathtakingly dangerous and intricate physical chaos that surrounded him. He was a former Vaudeville performer who grew up in a family act, and his body was a precision instrument for comedy. Keaton's films were masterclasses in physical storytelling and stunt work. In *Sherlock Jr.* (1924), he seamlessly leaps in and out of a movie screen, a piece of cinematic trickery that remains astonishing. In *Steamboat Bill, Jr.* (1928), he performs one of the most dangerous stunts in film history, standing perfectly still as the two-ton facade of a building collapses around him, surviving only because he is standing in the precise spot where an open window passes over him. Keaton's persona was a different kind of clown—one who didn't beg for the audience's sympathy but earned their awe. His impassive face was the ultimate mask, a canvas onto which the audience projected its own amusement and anxiety as he navigated a world determined to flatten him.

Completing the holy trinity of silent clowns were Stan Laurel and Oliver Hardy. As a duo, they perfected the classic clown pairing, a dynamic that stretched back to the clever and stupid Zanni of Commedia dell'arte. Stan was the whimpering, child-like innocent, the well-meaning fool whose simple-mindedness inevitably led to catastrophe. Ollie was the pompous, blustering authority figure, the self-proclaimed brains of the operation whose dignity was constantly being undermined by Stan's incompetence and the cruelty of fate. Their comedy was a slow burn, a meticulously crafted escalation of "tit-for-tat" destruction, as seen in their classic short *Big Business* (1929), where a dispute over selling a Christmas tree escalates until they have destroyed a man's house and their own car. Their dynamic—the interplay between the foolish underling and the frustrated boss—was a perfect comic formula that they explored with brilliant subtlety and timing.

These celluloid clowns took the broad archetypes of the circus and refined them for the intimacy of the camera. They demonstrated that a raised eyebrow, a shy smile, or a deadpan stare could be just as powerful as a fall from a horse or a pie in the face. They made the clown a global superstar and cemented the character not just as an entertainer, but as a potent symbol of the little guy fighting against an indifferent and often hostile world.

The Darker Shade of Laughter: The Rise of Coulrophobia

For most of history, the clown, in his many forms, was a figure of fun, satire, and even sacredness. Yet, in the latter half of the 20th century, a sinister shadow fell over the painted smile, and the bringer of joy began to morph into a symbol of terror in the popular imagination. This phenomenon, often dubbed "coulrophobia" (an unofficial term for the fear of clowns), has deep psychological roots, but it was powerfully amplified by real-world events and the deliberate subversion of the archetype in mass media.

The psychological unease created by clowns stems from several factors. One is the concept of the "uncanny valley," a term coined by roboticist Masahiro Mori to describe the sense of revulsion people feel towards robots that look almost, but not quite, human. The clown's makeup, with its fixed, exaggerated smile and unnatural skin tone, places the clown squarely in this valley. The painted grin hides the performer's true emotions, creating a disturbing disconnect. We are hardwired to read faces for social cues, but the clown's face is an unreadable, permanent mask of glee, which can feel deceptive and menacing. This is compounded by the clown's inherent nature as a trickster. The Jester, Harlequin, and the Auguste are all defined by their chaotic and unpredictable behavior. While this is funny in a controlled context, the idea of an unpredictable figure with a hidden identity and a manic grin can be profoundly unsettling.

This latent anxiety was tragically ignited by real-world horror. In the 1970s, the case of John Wayne Gacy horrified America. Gacy was a seemingly respectable community member who, by day, entertained children at parties and charity events as "Pogo the Clown." By night, he was a prolific serial killer who tortured and murdered at least 33 young men and boys, burying many of them in the crawl space of his home. The revelation that a man who wore the mask of childhood innocence was capable of such monstrous evil created an indelible and toxic link in the public consciousness. Gacy did not just tarnish the image of the clown; he weaponized it, forever planting the seed that behind the painted smile could lurk the most unspeakable darkness.

Popular culture was quick to seize upon and amplify this new fear. The definitive moment came in 1986 with the publication of Stephen King's novel *It*. King's antagonist, Pennywise the Dancing Clown, was not a human killer but a cosmic, shape-shifting entity that preyed on the children of Derry, Maine, by taking the form of their deepest fears. It chose the clown as its primary disguise precisely because it represented a corruption of childhood trust and joy. Pennywise was the ultimate evil clown, a being of pure malevolence hiding behind a friendly facade. The novel, and the subsequent 1990 television miniseries starring a terrifying Tim Curry, cemented the evil clown as a premier bogeyman for an entire generation.

From that point on, the trope exploded. The Joker, a Batman villain who had existed since the 1940s as a prankish criminal, was reimagined as a far more terrifying figure of anarchic nihilism, most notably in Heath Ledger's Oscar-winning performance in *The Dark Knight* (2008). Ledger's Joker was a scarred, psychologically unhinged agent of chaos whose clown makeup was a terrifying war paint. This darker archetype has become a staple of horror films, haunted houses, and even music, with bands like Insane Clown Posse adopting a menacing clown persona. The fear reached a bizarre peak in 2016 with the "creepy clown sightings," a viral phenomenon where people in clown costumes were reported lurking in forests and on roadsides across the globe, creating a genuine moral panic. The clown, once a sacred fool, had become a modern demon, a powerful symbol of hidden threats and corrupt innocence.

The Global Fool: Clowns Without Borders

Even as the clown's image was being twisted into a figure of fear, another, more hopeful evolution was taking place. Harkening back to the clown's most ancient function—that of a healer and a social unifier—a new movement emerged in the late 20th century that sought to use laughter and play as a form of humanitarian aid. This movement saw the clown not as an entertainer or a monster, but as a therapist, an ambassador of joy, and a provider of psychological first aid in the world's most desperate places.

The philosophical father of this movement was Dr. Hunter "Patch" Adams. A medical doctor and social activist, Adams gained fame in the 1970s for his unconventional approach to healthcare, which treated the patient's emotional and spiritual well-being as being just as important as their physical condition. Central to his philosophy was the power of humor and joy as a healing force. Adams would often don a red nose and clown costume while doing his rounds, believing that laughter could reduce stress, build trust, and improve patient outcomes. In 1971, he founded the Gesundheit! Institute, a project aimed at building a free, holistic hospital integrated with art, nature, and play. Though the hospital was never fully realized in its original vision, Adams's philosophy and his annual clowning trips to orphanages and hospitals in Russia and around the world inspired a global movement in therapeutic clowning.

This inspiration led directly to the formation of Clowns Without Borders in 1993. The organization was founded by the Spanish clown Tortell Poltrona, who was invited by a children's advocacy group to perform for children in a refugee camp in war-torn Croatia. The response was so overwhelmingly positive that it became clear there was a profound need for this kind of intervention. Clowns Without Borders was born from this realization, built on the principle that every child has a right to laugh and play, especially those who have suffered trauma, displacement, and loss.

The organization sends professional artists into refugee camps, conflict zones, and areas affected by natural disasters. Their mission is not to deliver food or medicine, but to provide what they call "psychological relief." A Clowns Without Borders performance is a simple affair—a small group of clowns with minimal props and no spoken language, relying on the universal language of slapstick, mime, and music. In a place where children have seen unspeakable horrors and live in a constant state of stress, the arrival of the clowns is a radical break. For a short while, the children are given permission to be children again. The laughter they share helps to alleviate the symptoms of post-traumatic stress disorder, build community resilience, and restore a sense of normalcy and hope. The clowns, by being ridiculous and vulnerable, absorb the fear and sadness of the environment and transform it into shared joy.

This humanitarian work represents a powerful and poignant return to the clown's deepest roots. The therapeutic clown, like the Native American Sacred Clown, enters a space of solemnity and crisis and disrupts it with irreverence and play, reminding the community of its own humanity. Like the court jester, they bring relief to those living under immense pressure. This global movement demonstrates the enduring power and adaptability of the clown archetype. Whether on a stage, on a screen, in a hospital, or in a refugee camp, the clown continues to serve an essential human function: to hold up a mirror to our world, to subvert our expectations, and to remind us that even in the darkest of times, there is power, release, and profound healing in the simple, beautiful act of laughter.

CHAPTER THREE

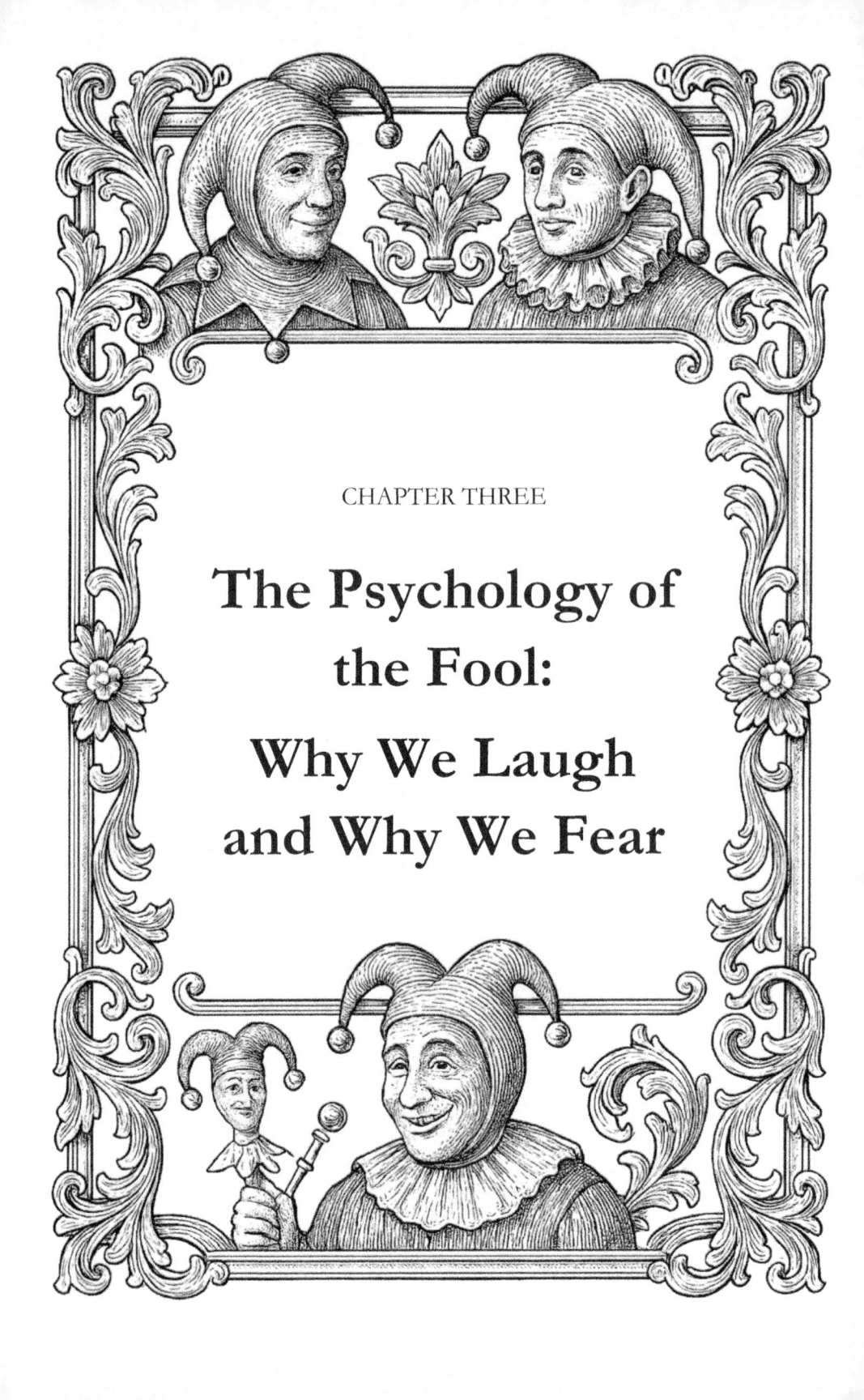

The Psychology of the Fool:

Why We Laugh and Why We Fear

To laugh at a clown is one of humanity's most primal and universal reactions. It is a response that transcends language, culture, and time. From the pharaoh's court to the modern circus ring, the sight of a fool tripping, tumbling, or simply being gloriously inept has provoked joy and mirth. Yet, for many, that same painted face and chaotic energy can trigger an equally primal, though opposite, reaction: a deep and unsettling fear. The clown occupies a unique and precarious position in our collective psyche, dwelling at the crossroads of comedy and horror. He is both a source of delight and a wellspring of anxiety, a dichotomy that cannot be explained by his actions alone. To truly understand the clown, we must look inward, into the complex machinery of the human mind.

The power of the clown lies not in the squirting flower or the oversized shoes, but in his ability to manipulate our fundamental psychological processes. Why do we find a pratfall so amusing? Why does a fixed, painted smile feel so menacing? The answers lie in ancient theories of humor, in the modern science of perception, and in the inherent tension between what we expect and what the clown delivers. This chapter delves into the psychology of the fool, deconstructing the cognitive and emotional mechanics that allow this single archetype to be both the funniest character in the room and, for some, the most terrifying. It is a journey into our own minds, exploring why we laugh at failure, why we crave order, and why the figure who so perfectly embodies chaos can be both a welcome release and a profound threat.

The Engine of Laughter: Superiority, Incongruity, and Relief

Laughter is a complex and still not fully understood human behavior, but centuries of philosophy and modern psychology have given us several powerful theories to explain why we find certain things funny. The clown, in his classic form, is a masterclass in activating all three major theories of humor: **superiority, incongruity, and relief.** His entire performance is a carefully constructed assault on our sense of order, logic, and social grace, and our laughter is the predictable, explosive result.

The oldest and perhaps most straightforward of these is the **Superiority Theory**, first articulated by philosophers like Plato and Thomas Hobbes. In its simplest form, this theory posits that we laugh at the misfortunes, follies, and inadequacies of others because it gives us a sudden sense of our own superiority. When we see a clown confidently attempt a simple task—like carrying a ladder or a bucket of water—and fail in the most spectacular way possible, we are witnessing a public display of incompetence. The clown trips over his own feet, gets tangled in the ladder, and inevitably soaks himself with the water. Our laughter, in this context, is a subconscious expression of triumph. We think, "I would not be so foolish. I know how to carry a ladder." This sudden glory, as Hobbes called it, is a primal and often cruel source of humor. The Auguste clown, with his bumbling nature and constant failures, is the perfect vessel for this kind of laughter. He is designed to be the fool, the one who gets things wrong so that we, the audience, can feel momentarily intelligent, competent, and superior. The slapstick, the pie in the face, the comical tumble—all are rituals of failure that elevate the audience by lowering the performer.

However, superiority alone does not explain all forms of

clown-based humor. A great deal of it stems from the **Incongruity Theory**, which suggests that humor arises from the violation of our mental patterns and expectations. Our brains are prediction machines, constantly trying to anticipate what will happen next based on past experience. Laughter is the pleasurable jolt we feel when that prediction is cleverly and harmlessly broken. The clown is a master of incongruity. He embodies a walking, talking paradox. His clothes don't fit, his props don't work as expected, and his logic is hilariously flawed. A tiny car pulls up and twenty clowns emerge from it. A flower, offered as a romantic gesture, suddenly squirts water. A violin, poised to play a beautiful melody, instead produces a honking sound. Each of these gags works by setting up a familiar expectation and then delivering a surprising, illogical, and nonsensical outcome. The gap between what we expect (a car holds four people) and what we see (a car holds twenty clowns) creates a cognitive dissonance that can only be resolved through the release of laughter. This is the intellectual side of clowning, the element that delights us with its cleverness and surreal creativity. It is the humor of the unexpected, and the clown is its most dedicated agent.

The third major engine of laughter is the **Relief Theory**, most closely associated with Sigmund Freud. This theory proposes that laughter is a way of venting nervous energy and releasing pent-up emotions and anxieties. Society requires us to repress our aggressive, sexual, and rebellious impulses in order to maintain social order. Comedy, and the clown in particular, provides a safe and socially acceptable outlet for these forbidden thoughts. The clown is a figure of pure id. He is anarchic, disruptive, and gleefully breaks every social rule. He throws pies at authority figures (the snooty Whiteface or the pompous ringmaster), makes a mockery of polite decorum, and generally creates chaos wherever he goes. When we laugh at his antics, we are, in a sense, vicariously participating in his rebellion. He is doing what we secretly wish we could do: defy our bosses, ignore social niceties, and create a glorious mess. The laughter that erupts is a release of the tension built up by our own self-control. The clown acts as our surrogate anarchist, and his performance is a ritual of liberation, allowing us to momentarily escape the constraints of civilized behavior.

Together, these three theories form a psychological trinity that explains the enduring power of the clown's appeal. He allows us to feel superior, delights us with his illogical creativity, and provides a safe outlet for our most repressed impulses. He is a perfectly calibrated machine for generating laughter, a testament to the fact that the art of the fool is deeply rooted in the fundamental workings of the human mind.

The Uncanny Valley: When the Smile Curdles

For every person who is delighted in the clown's antics, there seems to be another who finds the same figure deeply disturbing. The fear of clowns, or coulrophobia, is a very real and surprisingly common phenomenon. While this fear was undeniably amplified by media portrayals of evil clowns, its origins lie not in fiction, but in a fundamental quirk of human perception. The very things that are designed to make a clown friendly and amusing, the makeup, the fixed smile, the exaggerated features—are the same things that can trigger a profound sense of unease. This discomfort is best explained by the concept of the **"uncanny valley."**

Coined in the 1970s by roboticist Masahiro Mori, the term describes a specific point in aesthetics where an object that is meant to look human—like a humanoid robot, a mannequin, or a CGI character—becomes deeply unsettling precisely because it is *almost*, but not *quite*, perfect. Our empathetic response to human-like figures increases as they become more realistic, but it plummets into a "valley" of revulsion just before it reaches true human likeness. An object that is clearly a machine or a cartoon is not threatening. A real human is not threatening. But an object that blurs the line, that mimics humanity imperfectly, triggers a powerful cognitive alarm. It is a signal that something is fundamentally wrong.

The classic clown, with his painted face, falls squarely into this uncanny valley. The makeup is an attempt to create a simplified, idealized human face, one that is perpetually happy and non-threatening. However, the execution creates the opposite effect. The stark white base obliterates the natural skin tone, removing the subtle cues of blood flow and emotion that we rely on to read a person's health and intentions. The painted-on smile is the most significant offender. A real human smile is a dynamic event involving dozens of muscles, particularly around the eyes (a "Duchenne smile"). The clown's smile is a static, permanent grin, a rictus of joy that is not reflected in the eyes or the rest of the face. This creates a powerful emotional disconnect. The mouth signals happiness, but the eyes might be neutral or sad, creating a contradictory and untrustworthy expression. Our brains, which are expert at face detection, recognize the form of a human face but cannot properly read its intent. This ambiguity is deeply unsettling. Is this person truly happy, or are they hiding something malicious behind that painted mask?

This sense of unease is compounded by the exaggeration of other features. The oversized nose, the massive shoes, and the brightly colored wig distort the human form in a way that is unnatural. The clown's body does not move or behave like a normal person. He is clumsy yet surprisingly agile, a paradox of motion. This unpredictability, combined with the unreadable face, creates a figure whose intentions are impossible to gauge. The clown's entire being is a collection of mixed signals. He is dressed like a figure of fun, but his appearance triggers subconscious alarms about deception and artificiality. He is an imitation of a human, and a flawed one at that. For those who are particularly sensitive to these perceptual dissonances, the clown is not a funny character but a glitch in the human template, a walking, honking embodiment of the uncanny.

The Mask of Chaos: Anonymity and the Unpredictable Trickster

Beyond the unsettling nature of the clown's appearance, the fear he can inspire is also rooted in his fundamental identity as a trickster. From the Native American Contrary to the Italian Harlequin, the clown archetype has always been an agent of chaos, a character defined by his unpredictability and his defiance of social norms. While this is the source of his comedy, it is also the source of his potential menace. The clown represents a voluntary surrender of predictable, rule-based behavior, and this makes him an inherently powerful and potentially dangerous figure.

The makeup and costume function as a **mask**, and the mask is one of the oldest and most powerful tools of psychological transformation in human culture. Across civilizations, putting on a mask has been a ritual act that allows the wearer to shed their personal identity and adopt a new one, whether it be that of a god, a demon, or an ancestral spirit. The mask grants anonymity, and with anonymity comes a powerful sense of liberation from social consequences. The clown, by donning his painted face, is engaging in this ancient ritual. He is signaling to the world that he is no longer bound by the ordinary rules of conduct. He is free to be absurd, to be disruptive, and to be foolish.

For an audience in a theatre or circus tent, this is a safe and welcome form of chaos. The context is controlled, and we understand that the clown's anarchy is part of a performance. However, when the clown is removed from that context, his unpredictability becomes a threat. A clown seen on the street or in the woods, as in the 2016 "creepy clown" sightings, is terrifying precisely because he is an agent of chaos operating outside of the designated "play" frame. We have no idea what his intentions are. Will he offer us a flower, or will he do something violent? The mask hides his identity, and his role as a clown suggests his behavior will be erratic. This combination of anonymity and unpredictability is a potent recipe for fear. He is a wild card, a human question mark.

This fear is amplified by the clown's traditional relationship with children. The modern clown, particularly from the mid-20th century onward, was heavily marketed as a figure of childhood innocence and fun. This created a powerful association between clowns and a state of vulnerability and trust. The subversion of this relationship is therefore particularly jarring. The "evil clown" trope, as personified by Pennywise, is so effective because it is a direct betrayal of this trust. It takes a figure that is supposed to be safe and nurturing and reveals it to be a predator. This transforms the clown from a simple trickster into a symbol of ultimate deception, an entity that uses the mask of innocence to lure its victims.

Ultimately, the clown's power to both delight and terrify comes from the same source: his status as an outsider who operates beyond the normal rules of society. When we are in the mood for laughter and release, we welcome his chaotic energy. We see his foolishness as a joyful rebellion against the mundane. But when we are feeling vulnerable or anxious, that same chaotic energy feels like a threat. We see his painted smile not as an invitation to play, but as the deceptive mask of an unknowable and potentially malevolent force. The clown does not change; we do. He is simply the mirror, and what we see in his painted face—a hilarious fool or a terrifying demon—is often a reflection of our own state of mind.

CHAPTER FOUR

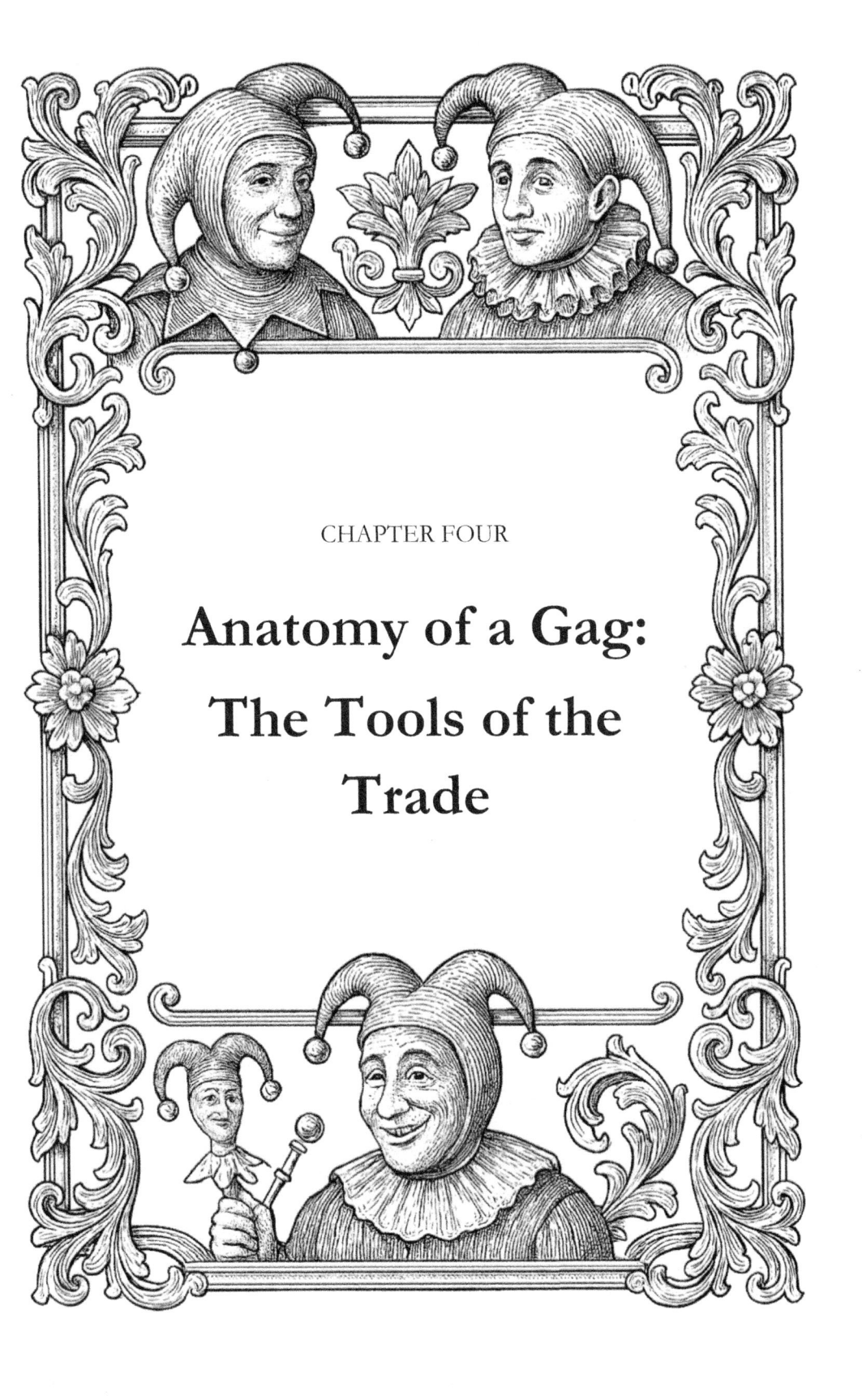

Anatomy of a Gag: The Tools of the Trade

The clown does not simply walk on stage; he arrives as a fully formed statement. Before he has uttered a sound or taken a single clumsy step, his very appearance has communicated a wealth of information to the audience. Every element of his presentation—from the arch of a painted eyebrow to the scuff on an oversized shoe—is part of a carefully constructed visual language, a toolkit of comedy refined over centuries of performance. This is the clown's great secret: nothing is accidental. The costume is a character sketch, the makeup is a mask of emotion, and the props are instruments of pure, calculated chaos. To understand the clown, one must learn to read this language and appreciate the history and purpose behind each iconic choice.

This chapter deconstructs that visual vocabulary. We will dissect the clown's uniform, piece by piece, to understand how these external elements build the internal character. We will explore the symbolic power of the three great faces—the Whiteface, the Auguste, and the Tramp—and see how a layer of greasepaint can define status, intelligence, and intent. We will trace the evolution of the clown's costume from the jester's motley to the modern circus jumpsuit, revealing how fabric and fit shape our perception of the fool. Finally, we will open the clown's prop trunk to examine the classic tools of his trade—the slapstick, the squirting flower, the tiny car—and uncover the simple, brilliant mechanics that make these gags timeless. This is an anatomy lesson in laughter, a look under the hood of the machine that makes us smile.

The First Canvas: Makeup and The Three Faces

The face is the primary instrument of human communication,

but the clown's face is something more: it is a billboard for his soul. Clown makeup, or "motley," is far more than simple decoration; it is the most important mask a clown will ever wear, establishing character, status, and comedic function before a single gag has been performed. This tradition of the painted face, stretching from the white-dusted visage of Pierrot to the garish grin of a modern Auguste, evolved into three distinct and archetypal forms in the American circus. Each face tells a different story and invites a different kind of laughter.

The **Whiteface** is the oldest and most aristocratic of the clown trinity. A direct descendant of the melancholy Pierrot and the revolutionary "Joey" of Joseph Grimaldi, the Whiteface clown is the master of ceremonies, the straight man, the intelligent (if often exasperated) leader of the clown troupe. His makeup is a statement of elegance and control. The entire face, and often the neck and ears, are covered in a smooth, perfect layer of clown white greasepaint. This creates a pristine, mask-like canvas, a symbol of high status and otherworldly detachment. Upon this white base, features are painted with delicate precision: thin, expressive eyebrows (often arched in surprise or disapproval), a neatly defined mouth, and perhaps a single, tasteful design like a teardrop or a beauty mark. The Whiteface does not distort the human face; it refines it into an idealized, almost porcelain form. This makeup style communicates intelligence and authority. He is the clown who knows the rules, even if he is about to watch his partners gleefully break them. His clean, clear features are designed for expression, allowing him to convey a range of emotions—from dignified annoyance to feigned shock—that drive the narrative of a gag.

In stark and glorious contrast stands the **Auguste**. If the Whiteface is the aristocrat, the Auguste is the anarchist, the bumbling fool, the lovable idiot whose every action results in chaos. Legend attributes his creation to a happy accident in 1860s Germany, when a clown named Tom Belling, flustered and new to the ring, allegedly tripped and smeared his face with dirt, delighting the audience with his clumsy, "auguste" (foolish) appearance. Whether true or not, the story captures the essence of the character. The Auguste's makeup is designed to be the opposite of the Whiteface's elegance. The base is not white but a flesh-tone, often a rosy, pink or tan, upon which exaggerated features are painted. Large patches of white are used to frame the eyes and mouth, making these expressive features pop from a great distance. The eyebrows are thick and unruly, and the mouth is often huge and upturned in a dopey grin. And, of course, there is the most iconic feature of all: the large, round, red nose. The red nose is the focal point of foolishness, a perpetual beacon of incompetence. The entire look is designed to communicate low status, clumsiness, and a complete lack of self-awareness. He is the troublemaker, the one who receives the pie to the face, the one who gets soaked with water. His makeup is a comic caricature, amplifying his expressive features to broadcast his foolishness to the back row of the biggest circus tent.

The third great face is the **Tramp** or **Hobo**, and it is America's most unique contribution to the art form. Born from the social realities of the late 19th and early 20th centuries—an era of itinerant workers, economic depression, and vast social displacement—the Tramp is a character of profound pathos. His makeup is designed not just to be funny, but to tell a story of hardship and resilience. The base is typically a flesh-tone, but a heavy, dark stipple on the lower face creates the illusion of a perpetual five-o'clock shadow, suggesting a man who hasn't had the luxury of a shave. The eyebrows are often painted with a worried or sad expression, and the mouth is downturned. A touch of red around the nose might suggest a man exposed to the elements or fond of cheap drink. This character was famously split into two schools of thought. There was the sad, pitiable Tramp, best exemplified by Emmett Kelly's "Weary Willie." Kelly's character was a portrait of failure, a perpetually forlorn figure whose attempts at simple tasks always ended in quiet defeat. In contrast, there was the "happy hobo" of performers like Otto Griebling, who maintained a cheerful, devil-may-care attitude despite his poverty. He was a survivor who found joy in his freedom, even if it was a freedom born of destitution. The Tramp's face is the most emotionally complex of the three, a mask that invites not just laughter, but empathy and a touch of melancholy.

So fundamental are these painted faces to the clown's identity that a unique tradition arose to protect them: the Clown Egg Register. Begun in the 1940s by Stan Bult, a member of Clowns International, this registry consists of painting a clown's unique makeup design onto a ceramic egg, creating a three-dimensional copyright of their persona. It is a charming and poignant tradition that underscores a deep truth: for a clown, their face is their legacy, their coat of arms, and the first and most important tool in their craft.

The Character's Skin: Costume and The Clown's Body

Once the face has established the character, the costume

must complete the story. A clown's attire is an extension of their personality, a second skin that reinforces their status, their worldview, and their comedic function. Like the makeup, the classic clown costumes evolved from a rich history of theatrical and social traditions, from the patchwork motley of the medieval jester to the distinct uniforms of the circus ring. Each element, from the fit of the suit to the shape of the shoes, is a deliberate choice designed to shape our perception of the character.

The historical ancestor of all clown costumes is **motley**. The iconic multi-colored, diamond-patterned suit of the court jester and the Commedia dell'arte Harlequin was more than just a vibrant uniform; it was a symbol of the clown's outsider status. Originally, the patchwork design was intended to represent the tattered, mended clothes of a poor servant, a man so destitute that his garments were a collage of scraps. Over time, this became stylized into the familiar diamond pattern, but its symbolic meaning remained. The jester was a man of "many parts," a figure who did not belong to any single social class or group. His costume was a visual representation of his fractured, liminal identity. He was a walking, talking mosaic, set apart from the uniform velvets and silks of the court.

When the clown entered the modern circus, this tradition splintered to match the new archetypes. The **Whiteface clown**, as the aristocrat of the ring, required a costume that projected elegance, intelligence, and authority. His uniform is the classic one-piece jumpsuit, often made of a shimmering, expensive-looking fabric like satin or lamé. The fit is crucial: it is well-tailored, allowing for graceful movement and acrobatic feats. The most significant feature of the Whiteface costume is the **ruff**, a large, pleated collar that encircles the neck. This is a direct nod to the fashion of Elizabethan and Jacobean nobility, as well as to the iconic costume of Pierrot. The ruff instantly signals high status and a certain classical refinement. The costume is often completed with a tall, conical hat, further elongating the body and adding to the air of dignity. The overall effect is one of competence and grace, which makes it all the funnier when the Whiteface's dignity is shattered by the antics of his chaotic partners.

The **Auguste's costume** is a perfect foil to the Whiteface's elegance. It is a celebration of chaos, bad taste, and poor tailoring. The suit is deliberately ill-fitting, either absurdly large and baggy or comically small and tight. The patterns are a riot of clashing colors: loud plaids are paired with bold stripes, and polka dots vie for attention with floral prints. The costume is designed to be an assault on the senses, a visual representation of the Auguste's muddled and anarchic mind. Every element is exaggerated for comic effect. The neckties are enormous, the suspenders are garish, and the jackets often have hidden gags, such as a flower that can be made to wilt on command. The Auguste's costume communicates that this is a character with no sense of propriety or style. He is a walking disaster, and his clothes are the first clue.

The **Tramp's costume** is, like his makeup, an exercise in pathos. He wears what was once a formal, dignified suit, now reduced to a tattered and well-worn shadow of its former self. It is often a dark color, like black or grey, but it is patched, torn, and covered in dust. The key to the Tramp's costume is that it tells a story of a fall from grace. This was once a man who had status, who owned a proper suit, but he has fallen on hard times. His costume is a failed attempt at maintaining dignity. He may still wear a tie, but it is crooked and stained. His shoes are broken, and he often wears fingerless gloves, a classic signifier of both poverty and a need to keep one's hands free for work. Unlike the Auguste's suit, which is comically mismatched, the Tramp's suit is tragically coherent. It is a single, sad statement about a life of hardship.

No discussion of clown costumes is complete without mentioning the **oversized shoes**. This iconic piece of footwear is more than just a funny accessory; it is a fundamental tool of physical comedy. The long, floppy shoes make normal walking a challenge, creating a natural and believable reason for the clown to trip, stumble, and fall. They are the foundation of his clumsiness. Psychologically, they complete the distortion of the human form, making the clown seem inherently unbalanced and ill-adapted to the physical world. They are the punchline to the joke that is the clown's body, a final, absurd touch that ensures he can never be taken seriously as a creature of grace or competence.

The Toolkit of Chaos: An Anatomy of Classic Props

If makeup is the clown's face and costume is his skin, then props are his hands, the tools he uses to interact with and disrupt the world around him. A clown prop is rarely what it appears to be; it is almost always a familiar object whose function has been cleverly and comically subverted. From the ancient slapstick to the modern rubber chicken, these props are the engines of the gag, the physical manifestation of the incongruity and surprise that lie at the heart of clowning. Each classic prop has a history and a specific comedic purpose, designed to exploit a particular psychological trigger in the audience.

The oldest and most fundamental of all clown props is the **slapstick**. Its history stretches back to the 16th-century Italian Commedia dell'arte, where the mischievous Harlequin wielded a simple wooden paddle called a *batocio*. This prop was ingeniously constructed from two thin slats of wood that were hinged at the handle. When an actor was struck with it, the slats would clap together, creating a loud, sharp "smack" that was far more dramatic than the actual impact. The slapstick allowed for the performance of energetic and seemingly violent comic fights without causing any real harm to the performers. It was the perfect tool for the anarchic, physical comedy of the Zanni. The prop was so central to this style of humor that it lent its name to the entire genre of "slapstick comedy." It represents the core of much clown humor: the safe, harmless, and hilarious presentation of violence and aggression.

Another classic prop that operates on the principle of subverted expectations is the **squirting flower**. This gag is a masterpiece of comic misdirection. The setup is a universal social ritual: a person, often the clown, offers another person a flower as a sign of friendship, romance, or apology. The flower, usually a lapel boutonnière, is a symbol of beauty and sincerity. The audience and the recipient of the flower are led to expect a pleasant, gentle moment. The punchline comes when the recipient leans in to smell the flower, and the clown, by squeezing a hidden bulb, squirts a jet of water directly into their face. The humor is born from the sudden, shocking violation of the social contract. The gesture of peace is revealed to be a prank. The squirting flower is the perfect prop for the mischievous Auguste, a tool that allows him to puncture pomposity and undermine sentimentality with a single, surprising squirt.

Where the squirting flower plays with social incongruity, the **tiny car** plays with physical incongruity. This gag, made world-famous by the legendary Ringling Bros. clown Lou Jacobs, is a pure sight gag that operates on the violation of our understanding of basic physics and space. The setup is simple: a ridiculously small car, often no bigger than a go-kart, drives into the center of the circus ring and putters to a stop. The audience chuckles at the absurdity of the vehicle itself. Then, the driver's door opens, and a single, full-sized clown emerges. This is followed by another. And another. And another. The stream of clowns emerging from the impossibly small vehicle continues until a dozen or more are standing around it. The gag works because it presents the audience with a visual paradox. Our brains know that the car cannot possibly hold that many people, yet we are seeing it happen before our eyes. The sheer, delightful impossibility of it creates a powerful and universal laugh.

Finally, there is the **rubber chicken**. Of all the classic clown props, the rubber chicken is perhaps the most purely absurd. It has no clear historical origin, likely emerging from the chaotic world of vaudeville, and it has no intrinsic function other than its own ridiculousness. A real chicken is a living, clucking animal. A cooked chicken is food. A rubber chicken is either. It is a completely useless and nonsensical object. Its humor comes from its sheer pointlessness. Why is the clown carrying a rubber chicken? There is no logical answer, and that is precisely why it is funny. The rubber chicken represents the moment when all logic breaks down, the pinnacle of surreal, incongruous humor. It is a symbol of comedy in its most distilled form: an object so inherently silly that its mere presence is enough to signal that the rules of reality no longer apply. It is the ultimate tool for a fool in a world that has, for a moment, gone completely mad.

OVERSIZED SHOES

RUBBER CHICKEN

SLAP-STICK

HONK HORN

FLOWER-SQUIRTER

CHAPTER FIVE

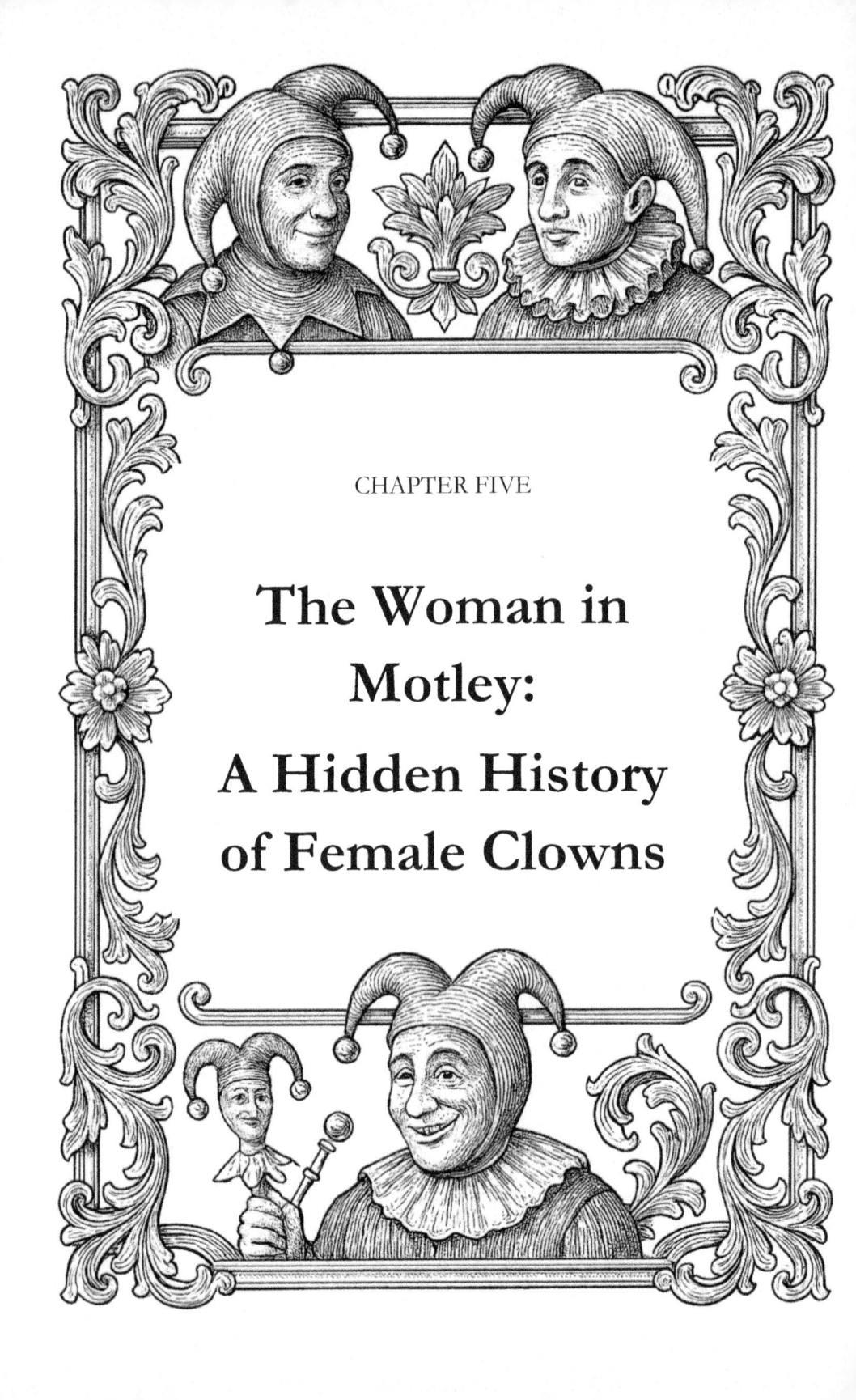

The Woman in Motley:

A Hidden History of Female Clowns

The history of the clown, as it is most often told, is a history of men. It is the story of male jesters whispering in the ears of kings, of the Fratellini brothers dominating the Parisian circus, of Chaplin and Keaton captivating the world from the silver screen. In this grand narrative, the woman in motley is often relegated to the wings—a footnote, an assistant, a pretty "clownesse" whose role is to be the graceful counterpoint to the male buffoon's chaotic energy. This telling of the story is not so much a falsehood as it is a profound omission, an oversight that has rendered a rich and courageous lineage of female performers nearly invisible. From the medieval courts to the modern stage, women have always been a part of the clowning tradition, not just as partners but as pioneers, innovators, and masters of the craft.

Their journey, however, has been fraught with unique challenges. They have had to navigate a world that often equated femininity with grace and fragility, qualities seen as antithetical to the boisterous, clumsy, and often grotesque nature of the classic clown. They have fought for the right to be not just beautiful, but foolish; not just charming, but chaotic. This chapter seeks to correct the record, to pull back the curtain on the hidden history of the female clown. It is a story of quiet infiltration and bold revolution, of women who donned the motley to subvert expectations, challenge gender roles, and carve out their own space in the sawdust ring and beyond. From the forgotten fools of the royal court to the godmother of modern clowning who built an institution to legitimize her art, the story of the woman in motley is a vital and powerful chapter in the long, strange history of the fool.

Jesters in Skirts and Queens of the Ring

While the official records of medieval and Renaissance courts are dominated by the names of male jesters, hints and fragments of evidence suggest that women, too, occupied the role of the fool. Their presence was often more precarious and their historical footprint far fainter, but they were there. In a world where a woman's public role was severely proscribed, the position of a "fool" or entertainer was one of the few avenues available for a woman to have a voice and a degree of autonomy, albeit a strange and risky one. These female jesters, or *folles*, are mentioned in court account books and literary texts. There was Jane the Fool, a jester in the court of Queen Catherine Parr, the sixth wife of Henry VIII, and later in the household of Mary I. Her role was likely less about sharp political satire and more about providing companionship and light entertainment, but she was a professional fool nonetheless, a woman paid for her wit and presence.

These early female fools had to walk an even finer line than their male counterparts. A man's impudence could be seen as daring; a women was often condemned as shrewish or immoral. Their humor was likely more subtle, their performances more musical or acrobatic, but their function was the same: to provide a release from the suffocating formality of court life. They were anomalies, women who existed outside the traditional roles of wife, mother, or nun, and in their own way, they were as disruptive to the social order as any male jester.

As the formal court jester faded and the circus rose to prominence in the 19th century, women began to find a more visible, if still highly circumscribed, place in the world of clowning. The early circus was a place of spectacle, and female performers were a key part of the attraction, primarily as graceful equestriennes, acrobats, and dancers. It was a natural, if slow, progression for some of these women to move into comedy. One of the first recognized female circus clowns in America was Amelia Butler, who began performing in the 1850s. She was celebrated for her charm and her skills as a comic rider, but her role was still defined in relation to the male clowns she performed with.

This became the dominant paradigm for the 19th-century "clownesse." She was typically young, pretty, and graceful. Her costume was a feminized version of the male clown's suit, often shorter and more form-fitting, designed to be attractive rather than absurd. Her function was not to be the primary buffoon, but to be the charming straight woman, the serene and lovely figure who would be the target of the male clown's pranks or who would set up his gags. She might perform a graceful dance, only to be comically interrupted. She might present an object of beauty, only to have it destroyed by a clumsy Auguste. Her role was to provide the "grace" that the male clown's "grotesque" could play against. While many of these women were talented performers and acrobats, the structure of the circus acts rarely allowed them to be the originators of the chaos. They were the passive recipients, the beautiful victims of the gag.

This is not to diminish their skill, but to recognize the powerful societal constraints placed upon them. The idea of a woman being genuinely clumsy, grotesque, or anarchic—the core attributes of the Auguste—was seen as deeply unfeminine and undesirable. Laughter is often predicated on a loss of dignity, and in the 19th century, a woman's dignity was a precious and fiercely guarded commodity. For a woman to voluntarily make herself a public object of ridicule was a radical and often unthinkable act. The few who did, like the celebrated British clown Lulu, an incredibly gifted acrobat and comedian who performed in the late 19th century, were exceptions that proved the rule. They were marvels, noted for their daring and for defying the expectations of their gender, but they did not, at the time, fundamentally change the template of the male-dominated clown alley.

Vaudeville Dames and The Subversive Gag

If the 19th-century circus placed female clowns in a restrictive box, the rise of vaudeville in the late 19th and early 20th centuries provided a crowbar to help pry it open. Vaudeville was a theatrical smorgasbord, a collection of disparate acting singers, dancers, comedians, magicians, acrobats, and animal trainers—all vying for the audience's attention on a single bill. This format was a boon for female performers. It offered them a stage where they could be the star of their own act, free from the narrative constraints of the circus ring. In the chaotic, fast-paced world of vaudeville, talent and originality were paramount, and women began to use comedy as a powerful tool of expression and, often, of subversion.

Vaudeville allowed women to craft their own comedic personas outside the rigid Whiteface/Auguste/Tramp archetypes. They could be wisecracking "dames," clumsy immigrants, or naive country girls, using humor to comment on everything from fashion and courtship to the burgeoning women's suffrage movement. Performers like Eva Tanguay, "The I Don't Care Girl," cultivated a wild, energetic, and slightly scandalous stage presence that was a form of clownish rebellion against the demure, corseted ideal of femininity. While not a clown in the traditional sense, her anarchic energy and her direct, sassy engagement with the audience were pure Auguste.

It was also in vaudeville that female physical comedians began to truly shine. The circus had demanded grace from its female performers, but vaudeville audiences delighted in a well-executed pratfall, regardless of who was performing it. Women who were skilled acrobats and comedians could now use their physicality for pure laughter. They could be clumsy, they could be awkward, they could engage in rough-and-tumble slapstick with male partners and often give as good as they got. This was a crucial step in breaking down the notion that a woman's body was too fragile or dignified for low comedy.

This newfound freedom in physical comedy paved the way for women to make their mark in the nascent film industry. While the silent screen was dominated by the likes of Chaplin, Keaton, and Laurel and Hardy, several talented women carved out careers as brilliant comediennes. The most significant of these was Mabel Normand. A frequent co-star and director for Chaplin and Roscoe "Fatty" Arbuckle at Keystone Studios, Normand was not just a pretty face; she was a gifted physical comedian and a comedic force in her own right. She could take a pie to the face with the best of them and was a brilliant improviser. She often played plucky, energetic heroines who were more than a match for their male counterparts, subverting the "damsel in distress" trope by being just as likely to start the fight as to be rescued from it. Her career was ultimately marred by scandal and tragedy, but her work in the silent era demonstrated that women could be the source, not just the object, of slapstick humor.

Even with these advances, the path was not easy. Female comedians often had to package their humor in a way that was deemed "safe" or "charming." They might play the "dizzy dame" or the "lovable scatterbrain," using a veneer of feminine ineptitude to make their wit and intelligence palatable to a society still uncomfortable with overtly clever or aggressive women. They were still, in many ways, playing a role, but it was a role they had a greater hand in writing. The vaudeville stage and the silent screen were crucial laboratories where the female clown learned to hone her craft, develop her voice, and prove that the art of the gag was not, and had never truly been, an exclusively male domain. They laid the groundwork for a revolution that would come to fruition decades later, a revolution that would be led by a woman who came not from the raucous world of vaudeville, but from the very heart of the traditional circus dynasty.

Annie Fratellini and the Modern Revolution

For much of the 20th century, the world of the European circus was dominated by a single, legendary name: Fratellini. The Fratellini brothers—Paul, François, and Albert—were the undisputed kings of the Parisian circus in the 1920s and 30s, a trio of clowns whose blend of music, acrobatics, and character-driven comedy set the standard for generations. Their legacy was a towering one, a patriarchal dynasty built on sawdust and greasepaint. It was into this world that Annie Fratellini was born in 1932, and it was she who would both honor that legacy and fundamentally revolutionize it, becoming arguably the most important female clown of the 20th century.

As the granddaughter of Paul Fratellini, Annie grew up immersed in the circus, but initially, she rejected the family trade. She became a talented musician and singer, finding success in the jazz clubs and music halls of Paris. The idea of becoming a clown, a role so thoroughly defined by the men in her family, held little appeal. The few "clownesses" she had seen were relegated to being decorative assistants, and she had no interest in playing a secondary role. The world of clowning, as she saw it, was not a place for a woman to be a true artist. It was a chance encounter with the filmmaker and clown Pierre Étaix that changed her trajectory. Étaix, who had worked with the great Jacques Tati, recognized in her a unique comedic potential, a natural vulnerability and timing that were the raw materials of a great clown. He encouraged her to reconsider her heritage, not as a burden, but as an opportunity.

Together, they began to develop a new clown character for her. In 1971, Annie Fratellini made her debut as a clown, but not as a dainty, graceful "clownesse." Instead, she created a classic Auguste character. This was a revolutionary act. She donned the traditional ill-fitting suit, the clumsy shoes, and the iconic red nose. Her makeup was a classic Auguste design, with a sad, slightly bewildered expression that instantly engendered sympathy and laughter. She played the saxophone badly, attempted tricks that invariably failed, and bumbled her way through routines with a heartbreaking earnestness. By embracing the low-status, foolish role of the Auguste, she shattered the long-standing taboo against women being genuinely clumsy, inept, and undignified on a public stage. She proved that the core of the clown character—its failures, its resilience, its sublime stupidity—was a universal human quality, not a masculine one.

Her partnership with Étaix, who performed as a classic, elegant Whiteface, created one of the most celebrated clown duos in European history. Their act was a perfect distillation of the traditional clown dynamic, but with a woman at the heart of the chaos, it felt entirely new. Audiences adored her. She was not a "female clown"; she was, simply, a great clown. Her success gave her a platform, and she used it to create an institution that would change the face of clowning and circus arts forever.

In 1974, Fratellini and Étaix founded the École Nationale du Cirque in Paris, the first professional, state-sponsored circus school in France. This was another revolutionary act. For centuries, circus skills had been passed down within families, a closed and often secretive tradition. There was no formal place to study the art of the trapeze, juggling, or, most importantly, clowning. The school legitimized the circus arts, elevating them to the same level as theatre, dance, and music. It opened up the profession to people from all backgrounds, regardless of their family connections.

Crucially, it opened the door for women. At the École Nationale du Cirque, women were not trained to be assistants; they were trained to be artists. They were taught the same skills, held to the same standards, and encouraged to find their own unique clown personas, just as the men were. Annie Fratellini herself was a guiding force at the school, a powerful role model who demonstrated through her own career that there were no limits to what a female clown could achieve. She was not just teaching routines; she was passing on a philosophy, one that viewed the clown as a vulnerable, poetic, and deeply human character.

The impact of Annie Fratellini and her school cannot be overstated. She reclaimed the art form for women, not by creating a new "feminine" style of clowning, but by mastering the classic tradition and proving that it belonged to her as much as it did to her celebrated grandfather. She professionalized the training, ensuring that future generations of clowns, both male and female, would be treated as serious artists. Her legacy is not just in her own brilliant performances, but in the countless women who were able to follow in her oversized footsteps, a new wave of female fools who would take her revolution and carry it forward into the 21st century.

The New Wave: Redefining the Female Fool

The revolution ignited by Annie Fratellini in the 1970s created the conditions for a global flourishing of female clowns. The establishment of formal training schools and the breakdown of old taboos meant that by the late 20th and early 21st centuries, a new generation of women were free to explore the full potential of the clown archetype, pushing its boundaries in ways that would have been unthinkable a century earlier. These contemporary female clowns are not defined by a single style; they are a diverse and powerful collection of artists who use clowning to explore everything from feminist theory and political satire to deeply personal storytelling and avant-garde performance art.

This new wave is characterized by a move away from the rigid circus archetypes and toward a more personal and often more vulnerable form of performance. Many contemporary female clowns, heavily influenced by the teachings of Jacques Lecoq and Philippe Gaulier, build their characters from the inside out. Their clown persona is not a separate entity but an amplification of their own quirks, fears, and joys. This has led to a style of clowning that is often more emotionally nuanced and thematically rich than traditional slapsticks.

One of the pioneers of this new approach is Nola Rae, a British performer who is often called the "grand-dame of clown-theatre." Trained at Lecoq's school, Rae's work blends mime, puppetry, and clowning to create silent, poetic, and often surreal theatrical pieces. Her characters are not circus fools but complex figures who navigate bizarre and dreamlike worlds. Her comedy is gentle and intelligent, drawing laughter from subtle character quirks and beautifully crafted physical storytelling rather than broad gags. She proved that a female clown could command a stage entirely on her own, creating a complete theatrical world through the power of her performance.

Another influential figure is the Canadian teacher and performer Sue Morrison, who developed her own distinct theory of clowning known as "Clown Through Mask." Her work emphasizes the clown as a social and shamanic figure, a being who connects with what she calls the "ecstasy of the idiot." Her training encourages performers, particularly women, to embrace their power and their rage, not just their playfulness. She challenges the notion of the clown as a purely gentle or pitiable figure, encouraging the exploration of a "fierce" clown, a powerful and disruptive force. This has opened the door for a style of female clowning that is confrontational, political, and unapologetically bold.

Today, the landscape is filled with a vibrant array of female clowns who are redefining the art form. Performers like the American-born, UK-based Deanna Fleysher, creator of the hit show *Butt Kapinski*, uses an interactive, improvisational style that breaks the fourth wall and turns the audience into co-conspirators in her chaotic detective story. Her clown is aggressively flirtatious and joyfully transgressive, playing with gender and power dynamics in a way that is both hilarious and thought-provoking. The duo behind the Australian troupe The Long Pigs created a dark, gothic form of clowning that explored themes of death and desire. These and countless other women are using the clown's mask of foolishness to speak profound truths about the female experience.

This new wave has effectively rendered the term "female clown" almost redundant. They are not defined by their gender but by the quality and originality of their art. They have proven that the clown's world is not limited to the traditional dynamics of the male-dominated circus ring. The female fool can be an aristocrat, an anarchist, a sad tramp, a political satirist, a fierce goddess, or a vulnerable poet. She has finally claimed her rightful place at the center of the ring, not as a decorative assistant, but as the master of the gag, the creator of the chaos, and the heart of the show. The woman in motley is no longer a hidden figure; she is a powerful and essential voice in the ongoing story of the fool.

CHAPTER SIX

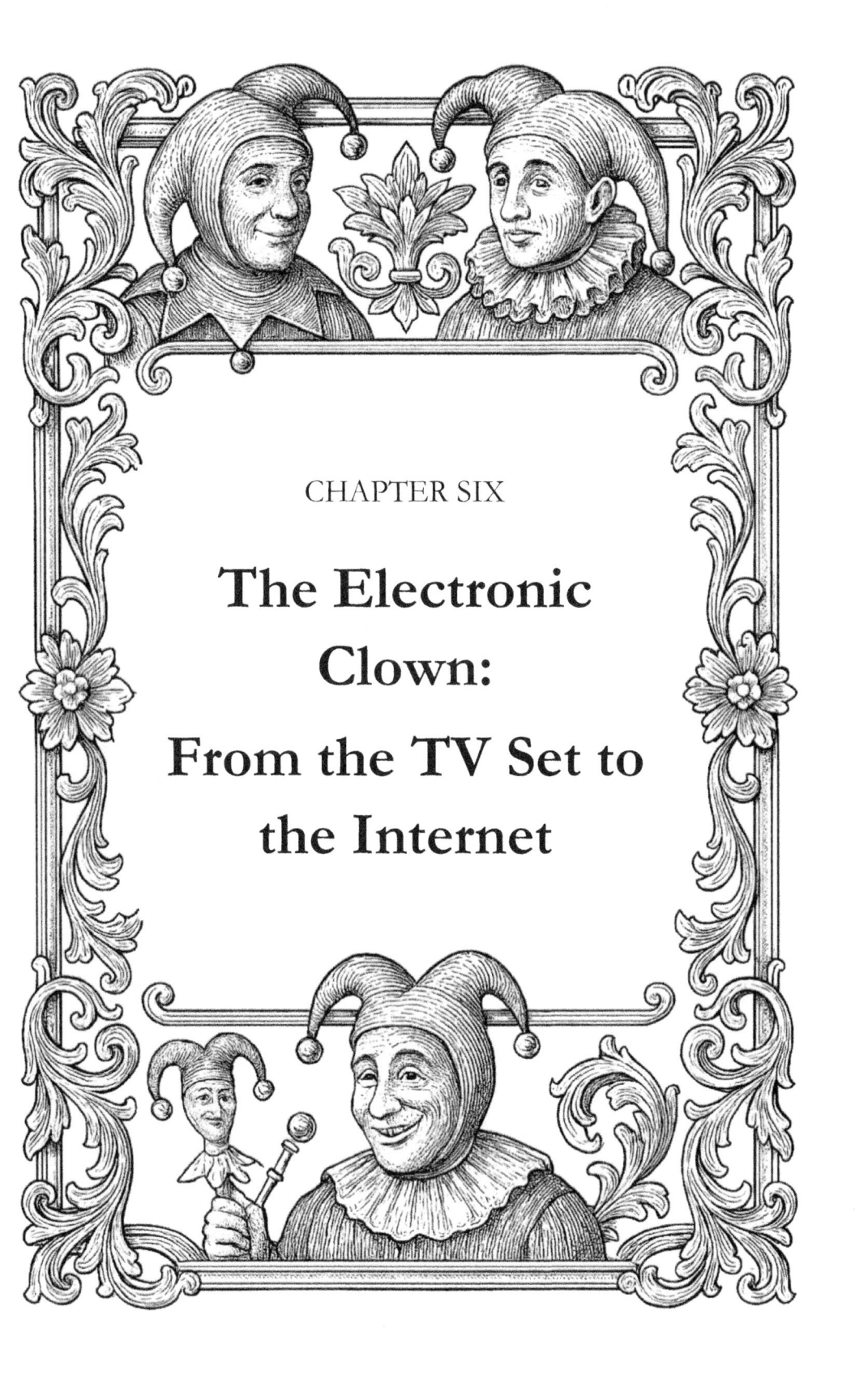

The Electronic Clown:

From the TV Set to the Internet

The sawdust ring of the circus and the flickering screen of the early cinema were transformative stages for the clown, but nothing in his long history could prepare him for the sheer, invasive power of the electronic age. The mid-20th century saw the dawn of television, a glowing box that would soon become the central hearth of the modern home. This new medium did not just offer the clown another stage; it offered him a direct, daily pipeline into the lives, homes, and formative minds of millions. The clown, once a special-occasion entertainer, became a familiar houseguest, a babysitter, a friendly face that beamed into living rooms across the nation every afternoon. This unprecedented intimacy would profoundly reshape the clown's identity, solidifying his role as a symbol of childhood innocence while simultaneously creating the conditions for his later, darker reinvention.

As television gave way to the internet, the clown's journey became even more surreal. He was no longer just a character in a controlled broadcast; he was a piece of data, an image to be endlessly copied, manipulated, and recontextualized. He became a meme, a viral sensation, a digital ghost haunting the new, unregulated public square of social media. This chapter traces the clown's dizzying odyssey through the electronic landscape. It is a story of how a character designed for the broad, physical comedy of the ring was repackaged for the small screen, becoming a beloved children's icon and a powerful corporate mascot. And it is the story of how that same icon, stripped of its original context, was warped and twisted in the funhouse mirror of the internet, becoming a symbol of everything from absurdist humor to genuine, widespread panic.

The Friendly Invasion: Clowns in the Golden Age of Television

In the years following World War II, as American society settled into an era of unprecedented suburban prosperity, the television set transitioned from a novelty for the wealthy to a ubiquitous piece of furniture. This new medium was hungry for content, particularly programming for the ballooning demographic of baby boomer children. Network executives and local station managers quickly realized that the clown, with his bright costume, simple gags, and non-threatening humor, was the perfect host for a children's television show. The 1950s and 60s thus became the golden age of the TV clown, a period when the character was sanitized, softened, and beamed directly into the heart of the American family.

The undisputed king of this new domain was **Bozo the Clown**. Bozo was not a single performer but a brilliant marketing concept, a franchised character whose rights were sold to local television stations across the country. Each city had its own Bozo, played by a local actor or television personality, but they all wore the same iconic costume: a blue jumpsuit, a ruffled collar, and a wild shock of red hair that framed a classic Auguste face. The format of *Bozo's Circus* was simple and effective, combining clown antics, cartoons, and a studio audience of excited children. The local Bozo was more than just a host; he was a trusted local celebrity, a friendly and slightly bumbling father figure who presided over an afternoon of fun. For millions of children, Bozo was their first and most formative encounter with a clown. He was not the sad, pathetic tramp or the anarchic trickster of the circus; he was a safe, dependable, and endlessly cheerful friend. This gentler, more paternal version of the clown became the dominant public perception, eclipsing the older, more complex archetypes.

While Bozo was conquering the local markets, another major figure emerged on the national stage: **Clarabell the Clown**, a key character on the wildly popular *Howdy Doody Show*. Played by Bob Keeshan (who would later become the beloved Captain Kangaroo), Clarabell was a fascinating evolution of the clown archetype. He was a silent clown, communicating only through mime, honking a horn, and, most famously, squirting a seltzer bottle at the show's host, Buffalo Bob Smith. Clarabell was a classic Auguste, a pure agent of mischief whose antics were a constant source of comic disruption. He was the playful id to Buffalo Bob's superego, but his silence made him endear rather than threatening. The show's most dramatic moment came in its final episode in 1960, when, for the first and only time, Clarabell spoke. Leaning into the camera with a tear in his eye, he uttered the show's final words: "Goodbye, kids." This moment was a powerful piece of television history, a poignant breaking of character that revealed the gentle man behind the painted face and cemented Clarabell's place in the hearts of a generation.

The success of these characters proved that the clown was a potent commercial force, a fact that was not lost on the burgeoning fast-food industry. In 1963, a Washington D.C. McDonald's franchise hired a local Bozo performer, Willard Scott, to create a new character to promote their restaurants. The result was **Ronald McDonald**, a character who would become one of the most recognized figures on the planet. The early Ronald was a more classic Auguste, with a cup for a nose and a food tray for a hat, his personality a bit more manic and clumsier. Over time, the character was refined and standardized, becoming the perpetually cheerful, magic-toting ambassador of the McDonald's brand. Ronald McDonald represents the ultimate commercialization of the clown. He was a character designed not just to entertain children, but to build brand loyalty from the earliest possible age. His friendly, non-threatening persona was a carefully crafted piece of corporate marketing, a symbol of happy meals and family fun.

The television clown, in all his forms, had a profound and lasting impact. He solidified the clown's image as an entertainer exclusively for children, stripping away much of the adult satire, social commentary, and pathos that had defined the character for centuries. He made the clown a safe, predictable, and commercially viable product. This very success, however, had an unintended consequence. By making the clown so ubiquitous and so closely associated with a sanitized version of childhood innocence, the television age created a powerful cultural symbol that was ripe for subversion. The friendly face of Bozo and Ronald McDonald became the placid surface beneath which a darker and more complex vision of the clown would eventually, and inevitably, emerge.

WHITEFACE
ELABORATE MAKEUP
REFINED
AUTHORITY

AUGUSTE
EXAGGERATED
FEATURES
BOISTEROUS

TRAMP
SHABBY APPEARANCE
WOEFUL
LOWEST STATUS

The Animated Buffoon: From Springfield to the Silver Screen

As live-action clowns were dominating children's television, a new and powerful form of media was beginning to explore the more satirical and dysfunctional aspects of the archetype: animation. Freed from the constraints of live performance and the need to be a friendly role model, the animated clown could be a more complex figure washed-up hack, a cynical entertainer, or a tragic figure of pathos. Animation allowed creators to deconstruct the clown, using the familiar tropes to tell stories that were often aimed at a much older audience.

No animated clown is more famous or more culturally significant than **Krusty the Clown** from *The Simpsons*. Krusty is a brilliant and biting satire of the Bozo-style television clown. On the surface, he is the beloved host of a children's variety show, with a forced laugh and a stable of tired gags. Behind the scenes, however, he is a deeply cynical, chain-smoking, gambling-addicted, and profoundly unhappy man. He is a walking paradox: a children's entertainer who seems to despise both children and entertainment. Krusty's character is a masterclass in exposing the weary reality behind the painted smile. He is not a monster; he is something far more relatable: a burnt-out professional going through the motions. His humor comes from the constant friction between his public persona and his private misery. He is a tragic figure, but his tragedy is played for laughs. Through Krusty, *The Simpsons* explores the commodification of joy and the exhaustion that comes from having to be "on" all the time. He is a post-modern jester, whose greatest joke is the sad, hollow reality of his own life.

While Krusty represents the cynical deconstruction of the TV clown, animation has also been used to explore the more poignant and artistic side of the archetype. The 2010 animated film *The Illusionist*, based on an unproduced script by the French comic genius Jacques Tati, is a beautiful and melancholic tribute to the dying art of the stage performer. The film's protagonist is a struggling magician, a character who shares much in common with the classic, gentle clown. He finds himself obsolete in a world increasingly dominated by rock and roll and television. The film is a quiet, meditative piece that captures the loneliness and dignity of the traditional entertainer in an age of mass media. It uses the visual language of animation to create a world of subtle beauty and profound sadness, a world where the simple magic of a stage performer is fading away. It is a powerful reminder of the pathos that has always been a part of the clown's DNA, from the silent longing of Pierrot to the weary sighs of Emmett Kelly.

The world of animation also provided a new arena for one of the clown's most enduring and terrifying alter egos: **The Joker**. While the character originated in comic books, his animated incarnations have been some of his most influential. In *Batman: The Animated Series* in the 1990s, Mark Hamill's iconic voice performance created a Joker who was a perfect blend of manic glee and genuine menace. He was a classic trickster, a "Clown Prince of Crime" whose gags were deadly and whose laughter was chilling. This version of the character was a pure agent of chaos who reveled in his own theatrical villainy. He was not a psychological case study; he was a force of nature, a modern-day Harlequin whose slapstick was played with acid-squirting flowers and lethal joy buzzers. This animated Joker reintroduced the concept of the dangerous, unpredictable fool to a mass audience, paving the way for the even darker live-action interpretations that would follow. Animation, with its capacity for expressive exaggeration, proved to be the perfect medium for capturing the full spectrum of the clown archetype, from the hilariously pathetic to the truly terrifying.

The Digital Ghost: Memes, Panics, and the Internet Clown

The dawn of the internet and the rise of social media in the 21st century represented the most radical shift in the clown's environment since the invention of the circus tent. The clown was no longer a character in a controlled performance or a curated broadcast; he became a piece of data, an image untethered from its original context, free to be copied, altered, and shared by millions of anonymous users. In the chaotic, unregulated ecosystem of the internet, the clown mutated into a new and often bizarre set of forms: the viral meme, the online troll, and the urban legend.

One of the first ways the clown was repurposed online was as a **meme**. The "creepy clown" image, already seeded in the culture by Stephen King and John Wayne Gacy, became a popular shorthand for anything unsettling or malevolent hiding behind a friendly facade. Images of Pennywise, or simply of generic, sinister-looking clowns, were used in countless image macros and reaction GIFs. The clown became a digital symbol, a quick and easy way to communicate a sense of dread or dark humor. This process flattened the character, stripping away his nuance and reducing him to a single, powerful signifier: "scary."

This digital reputation took on a terrifying real-world dimension in the late summer and fall of **2016**, with the outbreak of the **"creepy clown panic."** It began with isolated reports in South Carolina of people dressed as clowns attempting to lure children into the woods. Fueled by social media, these stories went viral, and a full-blown moral panic erupted. Suddenly, "phantom clown" sightings were being reported across the United States and then around the world. People created hoax social media accounts, posting threats against schools under the guise of a clown persona. Amateur pranksters donned clown masks and lurked on roadsides, filming the terrified reactions of passersby for YouTube. For a few months, the line between urban legend, internet prank, and potential real-world threat became terrifyingly blurred.

The 2016 panic was a perfect storm of anxieties. It combined a latent cultural fear of clowns with the viral amplification engine of social media and a 24-hour news cycle eager for sensational content. The clown became a blank screen onto which a wide range of societal fears were projected. The anonymity of the clown mask was a perfect metaphor for the anonymity of the internet, where anyone could adopt a persona to troll, threaten, or deceive. The clown lurking at the edge of the woods became a symbol of a world that felt increasingly unsafe and unpredictable. The panic eventually subsided, dismissed as a classic case of mass hysteria, but it left a lasting mark. It demonstrated how an archetype, supercharged by digital technology, could leap from the realm of fiction into a tangible and disruptive social force.

In a less menacing but equally surreal development, the internet has also given rise to a new kind of "clown" persona: the **online troll**. While not wearing literal greasepaint, the troll exhibits many of the classic traits of the negative clown archetype. They are agents of chaos who derive pleasure from disrupting conversations and provoking emotional reactions. They hide behind the anonymity of a screen name, using their mask of detachment to break social rules without fear of consequence. Like a jester using wit to undermine a courtier, the troll uses memes and inflammatory comments to undermine a reasoned argument. This "trolling" behavior, while toxic, is a modern, digital manifestation of the disruptive fool, a dark reflection of the clown's power to subvert order and mock sincerity.

From a trusted television friend to a viral harbinger of panic, the clown's journey through the electronic age has been a turbulent one. Mass media first simplified him into a symbol of pure innocence, and then the internet shattered that symbol, turning its fragments into tools for humor, satire, and fear. This evolution reveals a fundamental truth about the archetype: the clown is, and always has been, a reflection of the society in which he performs. In the age of the internet, an age defined by anonymity, viral phenomena, and the blurring of truth and fiction, it is perhaps no surprise that the clown has become our most prominent and unsettling digital ghost.

CHAPTER SEVEN

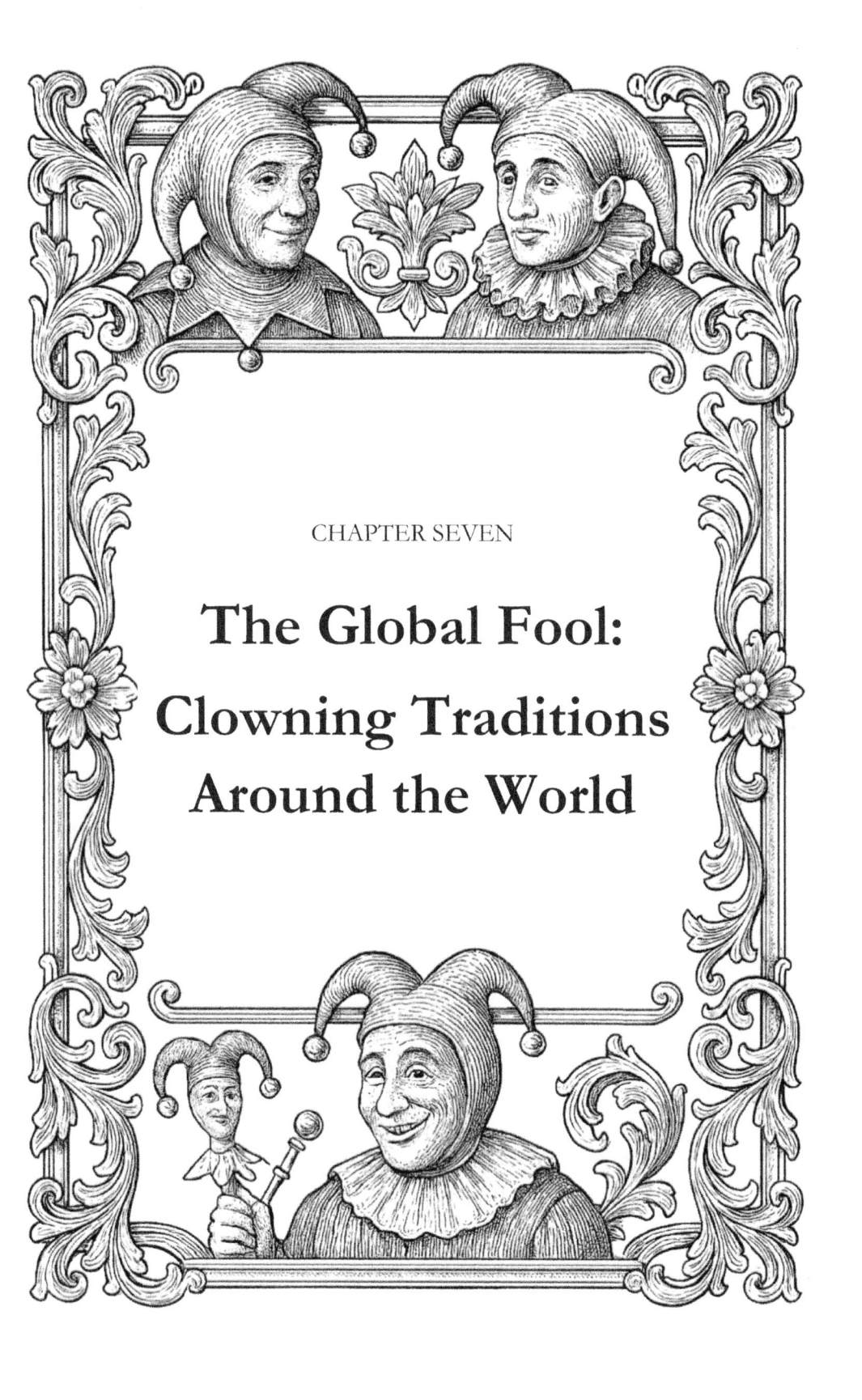

The Global Fool: Clowning Traditions Around the World

The familiar narrative of the clown—a direct line running from the Greek buffoon through the Italian Zanni and the English "Joey" to the American circus star—is a compelling one, but it is fundamentally incomplete. It is a story told primarily under a European and American lens, one that often overlooks the rich and ancient clowning traditions that developed independently all across the globe. The impulse to create a figure who stands outside the norms of society, who uses humor to critique, heal, and entertain, is not a Western invention; it is a human universal. From the courts of Indian maharajas to the vibrant festivals of West Africa and the stylized theatre of Japan, cultures everywhere have cultivated their own unique versions of the fool.

These global clowns, while sharing a common spirit with their Western counterparts, offer a fascinating diversity of form and function. They are not always found in a circus ring or a theatre; they may be central figures in religious rituals, political satire, or folkloric storytelling. Their masks are not always made of greasepaint, and their props are not always squirting flowers. Exploring these traditions is essential to understanding the true depth and breadth of the clown archetype. It reveals that the fool is a global citizen, a character who has been independently conceived and celebrated in countless societies. This chapter embarks on a journey beyond the Western world to meet these other fools, to understand their purpose, and to appreciate the many different masks that laughter can wear.

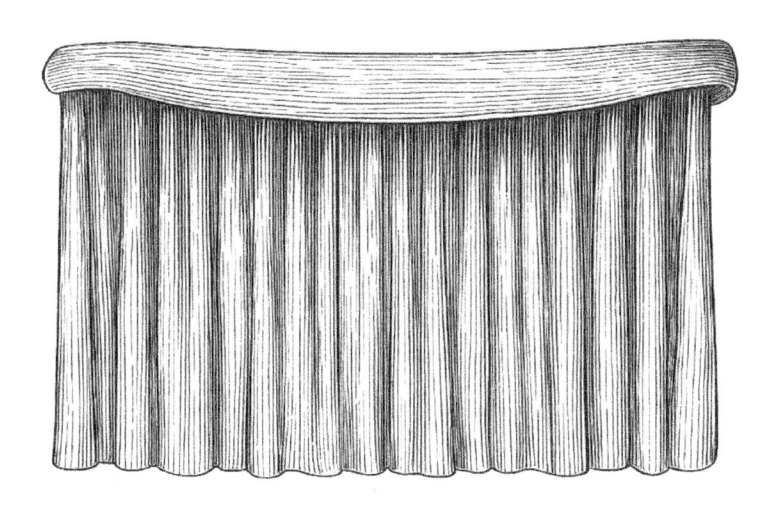

The Wise Fool of the East: India's Vidūṣaka and China's Jesters

Long before the Commedia dell'arte was formalizing its stock characters in Italy, a sophisticated and highly influential clown figure was already a central part of classical Indian theatre. The **Vidūṣaka** is a stock character in Sanskrit drama, a theatrical tradition that dates back to at least the 2nd century BCE. He is the loyal friend and companion to the noble hero of the play, typically a king or a prince. The Vidūṣaka is a Brahmin by caste, which should, in theory, grant him high social and religious status. However, he is a Brahmin who gleefully subverts all expectations of his station. He is portrayed as clumsy, greedy, gluttonous, and comically inept. His Sanskrit is often flawed, and he is far more interested in securing his next meal of sweets than in matters of state or spiritual enlightenment.

The Vidūṣaka's function is multifaceted. On the surface, he is the primary source of humor, his physical comedy and bumbling nature providing a lighthearted counterpoint to the often romantic and dramatic main plot. He is the hero's confidant, but his advice is almost always foolish and self-serving, leading to hilarious complications. Yet, beneath this veneer of buffoonery, the Vidūṣaka serves a deeper purpose. Like the European court jester, his status as a fool grants him a license to speak with a certain candor. He can gently mock the hero's lovesick pining or question a decision that others would not dare to challenge. He is a grounding force, a character whose obsession with worldly comforts—food, sleep, and safety—keeps the heroic, often otherworldly, passions of the protagonist tethered to a relatable human reality. His foolishness is a form of wisdom; by focusing on the mundane, he provides perspective and prevents the drama from becoming too self-important. He is not just a sidekick; he is a necessary balancing element, the comic earth to the hero's noble fire.

A parallel tradition of the wise-fooling jester also flourished in the imperial courts of **China**. For centuries, court jesters, known as *pái-yōu*, were fixtures in the palaces of emperors. Like their European counterparts, they were professional entertainers skilled in music, acrobatics, and witty banter. However, the most revered of these figures were those who used their humor not just to amuse, but to offer shrewd political advice and moral criticism. These were the scholar-jesters, men who combined the intellect of a court official with the license of a fool.

One of the most famous of these was Dongfang Shuo, a jester in the court of Emperor Wu of the Han Dynasty in the 2nd century BCE. Dongfang Shuo was a master of indirection. He would use riddles, parables, and elaborate jokes to critique the emperor's excesses or to warn him against a foolish policy. According to one story, when the emperor was considering expanding his massive imperial park, which displaced local farmers, Dongfang Shuo did not confront him directly. Instead, he told a story about a man on the brink of death whose only regret was not having lived in such a magnificent park. The emperor, understanding the satirical point—that the park was an extravagant luxury built on the suffering of his people—is said to have scaled back his plans. This method of "persuasion through jest" was the hallmark of the great Chinese court fool. He was a political artist, a man who had to be funnier and cleverer than the officials around him to be heard. His survival, and his influence, depended on his ability to wrap the bitter pill of truth in the sweet coating of a perfect joke.

The Trickster Spirit: Anansi and the Folkloric Clowns of Africa

In many African and Caribbean cultures, the clown archetype is not embodied by a human court jester or a stage performer, but by a powerful and enduring figure in folklore: the trickster spirit. These are not simply funny characters in stories; they are central figures in the cosmology and moral landscape of their cultures, divine or semi-divine beings who embody cleverness, rebellion, and the chaotic, unpredictable nature of life itself. The most famous and influential of these is **Anansi the Spider**.

Originating with the Ashanti people of modern-day Ghana, the tales of Anansi spread throughout West Africa and were later carried to the Caribbean and the Americas through the transatlantic slave trade. Anansi is a classic trickster. He is a small, seemingly powerless creature who must survive in a world of much larger and more powerful beings. He does so not through strength, but through his extraordinary cunning, wit, and verbal dexterity. Anansi is the ultimate underdog, constantly hatching elaborate schemes to outsmart his opponents, who often include formidable figures like the Sky God Nyame, tigers, and snakes. He is the keeper of all stories, having famously tricked the Sky God into giving them to him to share with humanity.

Anansi is a complex and morally ambiguous figure. He is at once a culture hero, a creative force who brings knowledge and stories to the world, and a selfish, greedy buffoon whose schemes often backfire in hilarious ways. He is a liar, a thief, and a glutton, but his cleverness is celebrated. The Anansi tales are told not just for entertainment, but for instruction. They are cautionary tales about the dangers of greed and arrogance, but they are also lessons in strategy and resilience. For the enslaved Africans in the New World, Anansi became a potent symbol of resistance. He was the small creature who could outwit the powerful master, a figure whose triumphs provided a psychological outlet and a source of hope. His trickery was a form of rebellion, his laughter a tool of survival. Anansi embodies the spirit of the clown as a survivor, a being who uses intelligence and humor to navigate and subvert an oppressive world.

Beyond the folkloric tradition, many African cultures have rich traditions of ritual clowning, often involving masked performers in religious ceremonies and community festivals. Among the Dogon people of Mali, masked dancers known as the *Awa* perform elaborate rituals to bridge the gap between the human and spirit worlds. Within these serious ceremonies, certain masked figures are permitted to engage in disruptive, comic, and often obscene behavior. These ritual clowns will mock the other dancers, harass onlookers, and generally create a zone of chaos within the sacred space. Like the Native American Sacred Clown, their purpose is not to desecrate the ritual, but to invigorate it. Their foolishness serves to release tension, to engage the community, and to remind everyone that the spiritual world is not just solemn and orderly, but also wild, unpredictable, and filled with a powerful, creative energy.

From Noh to Kabuki: The Comic Masks of Japan

The highly stylized and traditional world of Japanese theatre may seem an unlikely place to find a clown, but comic figures have always been an essential component of its major forms, from the stately Noh to the flamboyant Kabuki. Japanese clowns, however, are rarely the chaotic, independent agents seen in the West. Instead, their foolishness is a carefully choreographed and highly integrated part of a much larger aesthetic and dramatic structure.

In the medieval **Noh** theatre, a deeply symbolic and minimalist art form, the comic relief is provided by the *kyōgen* actor. Noh plays are typically serious, mythic tales of gods, ghosts, and warriors. Between these solemn plays, a separate, short comic play called a kyōgen would be performed. The word *kyōgen* translates to "mad words" or "wild speech," and these plays feature stock characters like the bumbling servant, the pretentious but ignorant master, and the clever trickster. The humor is often satirical, poking fun at human vanity and foolishness. The kyōgen actor also sometimes appears within the Noh play itself, often as a commoner or peasant who provides a simple, rustic perspective on the grand, mythic events unfolding. His role is to be the humanizing element, the touch of earthy reality that keeps the ethereal world of Noh grounded.

In the more spectacular and popular **Kabuki** theatre, which emerged in the 17th century, the clown's DNA can be seen in the stock character of the *sarumawashi*, or "monkey-trainer." More broadly, the comic roles in Kabuki are known as *dōkegata*. These characters are not always central to the plot, but they provide crucial moments of levity in the often long and dramatic plays. Their comedy is highly physical, involving exaggerated movements, comical facial expressions (aided by the dramatic *kumadori* makeup), and witty, often pun-filled, wordplay. Like the Vidūṣaka of India, the Kabuki clown is often a servant or a minor official whose foolishness serves to highlight the seriousness and nobility of the samurai heroes. He is a master of timing, able to inject a moment of laughter into a tense scene without breaking the overall dramatic tone.

One of the most fascinating aspects of the Japanese comic tradition is its emphasis on failure and incompetence. The kyōgen character of Tarō Kaja, the bumbling servant, is a master of misunderstanding his master's orders, with disastrously funny results. This celebration of failure is a core component of clowning worldwide, but in the highly structured and honor-bound society of feudal Japan, the figure of the fool provided a particularly important social release valve. The clown was the one character who was allowed to fail, to be incompetent, to lose face without bringing shame. His foolishness was a necessary counterpoint to the rigid codes of honor that governed the lives of the samurai and the nobility. He was a living, breathing demonstration of human imperfection in a culture that strove for perfection, and the laughter he provoked was a vital acknowledgment of that shared, flawed humanity.

CHAPTER EIGHT

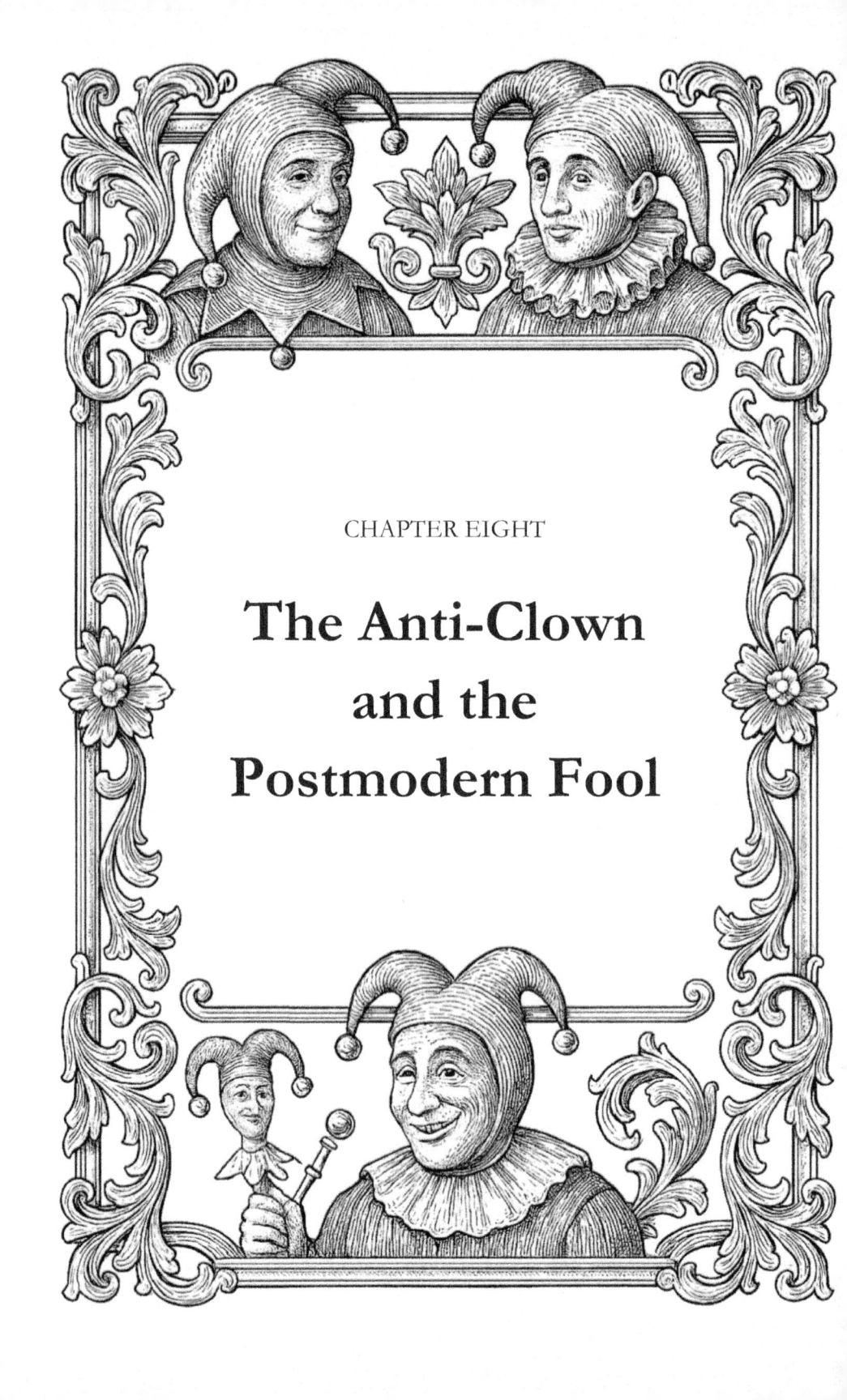

The Anti-Clown and the Postmodern Fool

By the latter half of the 20th century, the classic clown, with his earnest pratfalls and predictable gags, began to seem increasingly out of step with the times. In a world grappling with the Vietnam War, political assassinations, and a growing sense of societal disillusionment, the simple innocence of a Bozo or the charming pathos of a Chaplin Tramp felt like relics from a bygone era. The cultural landscape was becoming more cynical, more self-aware, and more fragmented. It was in this environment of irony and skepticism that a new kind of fool began to emerge: the anti-clown. This was a performer who wore the mask of the clown not to bring simple joy, but to provoke, confuse, and challenge the very nature of performance itself.

The anti-clown deconstructs the traditional clowning contract. Where the classic clown's goal is to make the audience comfortable through laughter, the anti-clown's goal is often to make them profoundly uncomfortable through ambiguity and confrontation. The postmodern fool is not interested in telling a joke; he is interested in examining the joke, taking it apart to see how it works, and often leaving the audience with the unassembled pieces. This chapter delves into the strange and fascinating world of this deconstructed fool. It is a journey into the heart of performance art, political satire, and philosophical nihilism, exploring how the ancient figure of the clown was repurposed by a modern world obsessed with questioning authenticity, meaning, and reality itself. From the bewildering anti-humor of Andy Kaufman to the terrifying nihilism of the modern Joker, this is the story of how the fool stopped trying to be funny and started trying to be true.

The Kaufman Effect: Comedy as Performance Art

No single figure embodies the spirit of the anti-clown more perfectly or more bafflingly than Andy Kaufman. He was a performer who was often labeled a comedian, but he famously hated that designation. He did not tell jokes, and his primary goal was not always to make people laugh. His art was the performance itself, and his true medium was the audience's perception of reality. Kaufman was a master of blurring the line between character and self, between the stage and real life, to the point where no one—not his fellow performers, not the network executives, and certainly not the audience—was ever entirely sure what was real and what was part of the act. He did not just play the fool; he weaponized foolishness to create a state of genuine, often uncomfortable, confusion.

Kaufman's gallery of characters was a collection of brilliant deconstructions of classic performance tropes. He first gained national attention with his **"Foreign Man"** character. With a thick, unplaceable accent and a painfully shy demeanor, Foreign Man would come on stage and tell a series of terrible, rambling jokes, punctuated by the nervous catchphrase, "Tenk you veddy much." The audience would laugh, but it was a laughter rooted in superiority. They were laughing at this awkward, incompetent fool. Then, just as the audience had settled into this comfortable dynamic, Foreign Man would announce he was going to do his "imitation of de Elvis Presley." What followed was a stunningly accurate, powerful, and charismatic impersonation of Elvis. The audience would erupt in applause, not just for the quality of the impersonation, but because they realized the "fool" they had been laughing at was, in fact, a brilliant and charismatic performer. The gag was on them. Kaufman manipulated their sense of superiority and then shattered it, forcing them to question their own initial judgments.

Even more confrontational was his creation of **Tony Clifton**, a boorish, third-rate Las Vegas lounge singer. With a cheap tuxedo, a ruffled shirt, a prosthetic paunch, and a thick mustache, Clifton was an aggressively untalented and deeply unpleasant character who would insult his audience and sing poorly. The genius of the character, however, was in Kaufman's insistence that Clifton was a real person. He refused to admit he was playing a role. He would hire other actors to play Clifton in public, further muddying the waters. He once had Clifton open for him at a concert, leading to a bizarre on-stage argument between the two. He even managed to get Tony Clifton guest-starring roles on television shows like *Taxi*, where his disruptive and abusive behavior inevitably got him fired, an event that was then reported in the press as a real conflict. By treating the mask as a separate reality, Kaufman was not just creating a character; he was creating a social experiment. He was exploring the nature of identity and celebrity, proving that if a performer commits to a fiction with enough conviction, he can bend reality around it. The audience was not in on the joke; they were the subject of it. In other performances, he would simply appear on stage and read aloud from *The Great Gatsby* until the audience members, bored and frustrated, began to leave. This was anti-humor in its purest form, a deliberate refusal to meet the most basic expectation of a performer: to entertain.

Kaufman's most controversial act was his foray into **inter-gender wrestling**. He declared himself the "Inter-Gender Wrestling Champion of the World" and offered a cash prize to any woman who could pin him. This was performance art at its most provocative. The act generated genuine hatred. Feminist groups protested, and his televised wrestling matches with a professional male wrestler, Jerry "The King" Lawler, culminated in a notorious on-air brawl on *Late Night with David Letterman*. For years, the public debated whether his feud with Lawler was real or staged. It was, of course, a brilliant piece of performance art, a collaboration between the two men designed to create the perfect illusion of reality television decades before the genre existed. Kaufman, as the chauvinistic wrestling clown, was holding up a mirror to the absurdity of professional wrestling and the ugliest aspects of American masculinity. He was willing to be hated, to be seen as a villain, in service of his art. His goal was not to entertain in the traditional sense, but to elicit a genuine emotional response, whether it was laughter, pity, confusion, or pure rage. He was the ultimate postmodern fool, a trickster whose greatest prank was on the very concept of an authentic self.

The Political Fool: Clowning as Activism and Confrontation

While Andy Kaufman was deconstructing the art of performance, other groups were harnessing the clown's disruptive power for more explicitly political ends. The jester's ancient license to mock power was rediscovered and repurposed by activists who understood that absurdity could be a more effective weapon than aggression. By adopting the mask of the clown, these political fools were able to confront authority, de-escalate tension, and expose the inherent ridiculousness of militarism and state control.

This tradition has its modern roots in the counter-culture

movements of the 1960s. Groups like the **Yippies** (Youth International Party), co-founded by activists like Abbie Hoffman and Jerry Rubin, used clownish street theatre and surreal pranks to protest the Vietnam War and the political establishment. Their tactics were pure jester-like disruption. In 1967, they organized a demonstration to try and "levitate" the Pentagon using psychic energy. In 1968, they nominated a pig named Pigasus the Immortal for President of the United States at the chaotic Democratic National Convention in Chicago. These were not serious political proposals; they were acts of satirical warfare. By responding to the grim reality of war and political corruption with carnivalesque absurdity, the Yippies highlighted the insanity of the establishment itself. They were using the fool's immunity to logic to stage a powerful critique, proving that sometimes the most serious political statement is a well-timed, ridiculous joke.

This philosophy of clowning as a form of non-violent resistance has been refined and organized in more recent times by groups like the **Clandestine Insurgent Rebel Clown Army (CIRCA)**. Founded in the United Kingdom in 2003 to protest the impending invasion of Iraq, CIRCA adopted the clown persona as a form of radical political identity. Their members dress in a style that is a cross between military fatigue and a clown costume, a visual paradox that is central to their philosophy. They operate on the principle that the clown's vulnerability, foolishness, and joy are potent tools for disarming confrontation.

Their tactics are a form of psychological jujitsu. During tense protests, a "clown army" will march in absurd, mock-military formations. They will confront lines of heavily armed riot police not with rocks or insults, but with feather dusters to "clean" their uniforms, with offers of flowers, or by blowing bubbles. This creates a powerful cognitive dissonance for both the police and onlookers. A police officer is trained to respond to aggression with controlled force. They are not trained to respond to a clown trying to engage them in a tickle-fight. The clown's actions are deliberately non-threatening and ludicrous, which serves to de-escalate a potentially violent situation. At the same time, this confrontation highlights the absurdity of the state's display of force. The image of a stoic, helmeted officer being offered a rubber chicken by a smiling clown is a powerful piece of political theatre. It reframes the conflict, shifting it from a battle of force to a battle of ideas, a battle of the heavily armed but inflexible state apparatus is ill-equipped to win. The rebel clown army uses its own joyful foolishness to expose the tragic foolishness of war and violence.

The Nihilist in Greasepaint: The Modern Joker and the Absence of Meaning

If the political clown represents the fool as a force for social change, another, darker evolution was taking place in popular culture, one that took the clown's disruptive nature to its ultimate, nihilistic conclusion. This evolution is best seen in the modern reimagining of Batman's arch-nemesis, **The Joker.** The character, who began his life in the 1940s as a relatively straightforward (if theatrical) criminal prankster, has been transformed over the decades into a terrifying symbol of philosophical anarchy, a clown who seeks not just to break the rules, but to prove that rules themselves are a meaningless joke.

This transformation reached its zenith with Heath Ledger's posthumously Oscar-winning performance in the 2008 film *The Dark Knight*. Ledger's Joker is the ultimate anti-clown, a being who has stripped away all the comforting elements of the archetype and left only the terrifying core of pure, unadulterated chaos. His clown makeup is not the neat, professional motley of a circus performer; it is a smeared, cracking, and deeply unsettling war paint, a crude mask that seems to have been applied to hide not just his identity, but a profound psychological wound.

The terror of this Joker lies in his complete rejection of the logic that governs both society and storytelling. He is a character without a comprehensible motive. When asked why he wants to create chaos, he doesn't offer a plan for world domination or financial gain; he simply describes himself as a "dog chasing cars" who "just does things." The film deliberately denies the audience the comfort of a backstory. The Joker tells multiple, contradictory stories about how he got his facial scars, at one point claiming his father inflicted them, at another that he did it to himself. This refusal to provide a clear story is a brilliant piece of postmodern villainy. It prevents us from psychologizing him, from reducing his evil to a simple case of trauma. He is not a product of his environment; he is an elemental force, a self-creating agent of chaos.

His "gags" are not designed to be funny to anyone but himself. He sets fire to a mountain of cash, not to make a point, but simply to prove that some men "just want to watch the world burn." His most famous "magic trick" involves making a pencil "disappear" by slamming a man's head onto it. This is the humor of pure malevolence, a terrifying inversion of the clown's traditional role. The classic clown uses a harmless prank to puncture pomposity; this Joker uses a lethal one to demonstrate the fragility of life. His ultimate philosophical goal is to prove to the citizens of Gotham—and by extension, the audience—that their codes of ethics, their laws, and their belief in order are a "bad joke," a thin veneer of civility that will crack under the slightest pressure. He is the fool who has stared into the abyss and has come back laughing, not with joy, but with the terrifying glee of someone who has realized that nothing matters. He is the clown as a philosophical black hole, a walking, cackling embodiment of the absence of meaning. This portrayal represents the most extreme deconstruction of the archetype, transforming the jester who speaks truth to power into a terrifying prophet who insists that there is no truth at all.

CHAPTER NINE

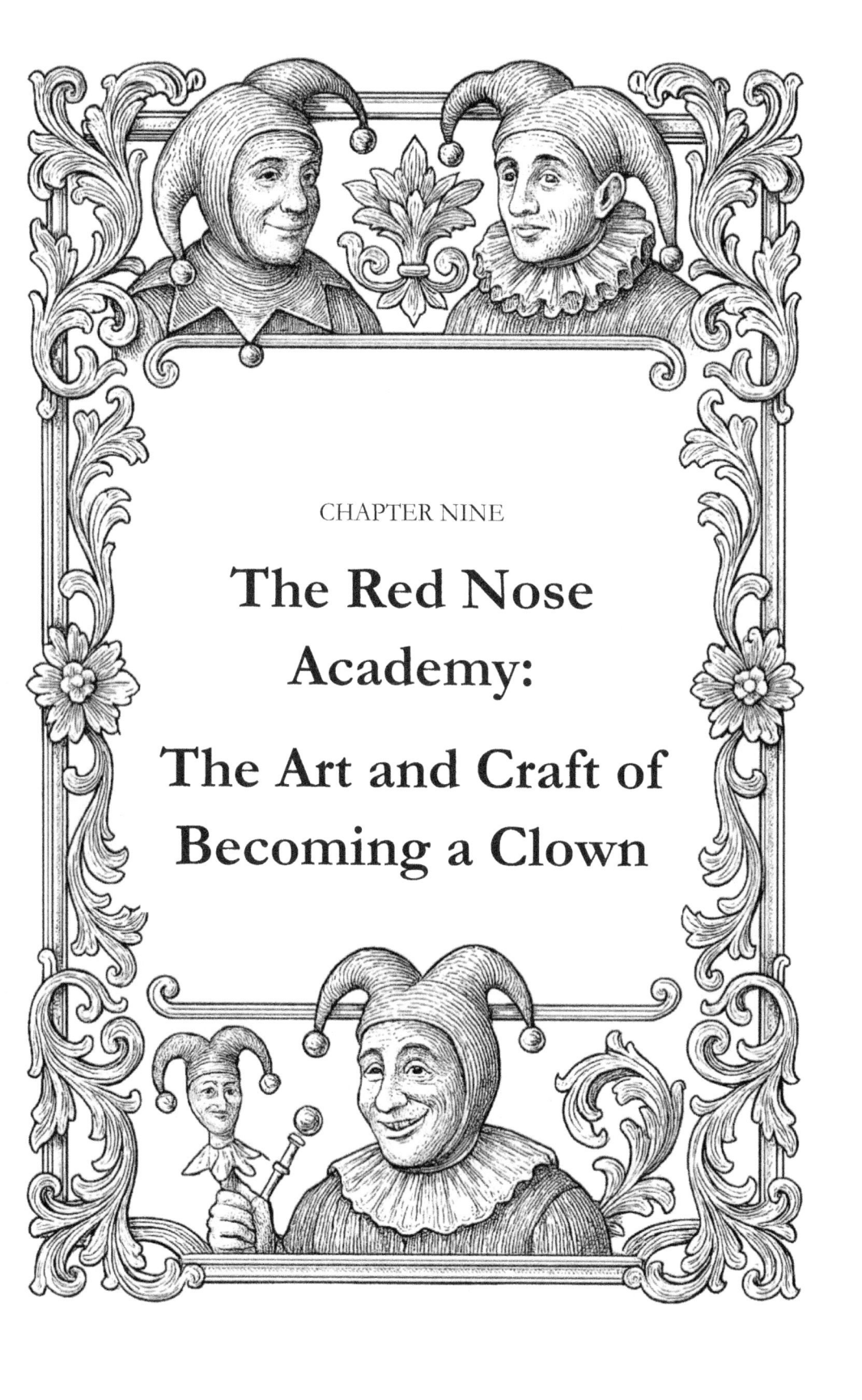

The Red Nose Academy:

The Art and Craft of Becoming a Clown

To the uninitiated, the art of the clown can seem like a happy accident, a natural talent for silliness that one is either born with or not. We watch a performer tumble, honk a horn, or take a pie to the face and assume it is the result of simple, uninhibited playfulness. This perception, however, belies a deep and rigorous truth: behind every great clown is a foundation of immense discipline, intense training, and a profound understanding of the craft. The sublime stupidity of a master fool is not a gift; it is an achievement. Becoming a clown is not about learning to tell jokes or juggle; it is a transformative process of stripping away inhibitions, mastering the body, and, most importantly, discovering the unique, vulnerable, and hilarious fool that resides within.

In the 20th century, as clowning was increasingly recognized as a serious art form, specialized schools emerged to teach its secrets. These were not places for learning simple gags, but laboratories for exploring the very essence of human comedy. From the hallowed halls of Parisian theatre schools to the raucous, practical world of the American circus college, these "red nose academies" developed distinct and powerful philosophies for training the modern fool. This chapter pulls back the curtain on this hidden world of clown education. We will explore the influential methods of the great European masters, who saw the clown as a poetic and personal creation. We will contrast this with the pragmatic, skills-based approach of the American circus, which trained clowns to be effective entertainers for a mass audience. And we will uncover the core curriculum that unites all these traditions: the embrace of failure, the search for a personal persona, and the unwavering dedication required to turn incompetence into a high art.

The Architect of Play: The Lecoq Method and the Neutral Mask

In the heart of Paris, far from the sawdust and spectacle of the circus, a quiet revolution in physical theatre was taking place that would forever change how clowns are trained. At L'École Internationale de Théâtre Jacques Lecoq, the French master Jacques Lecoq (1921-1999) developed a pedagogical method that treated the body as the primary source of all theatrical creation. Lecoq was not interested in teaching a particular style of acting; he was interested in preparing the actor's body to be a blank slate, a "neutral" instrument ready to discover and embody any character or form. For Lecoq, the clown was not a character to be put on like a costume, but a fundamental state of being to be discovered within the performer. His school became the intellectual and physical wellspring for a new generation of theatrical clowns.

The journey of a Lecoq student began not with a red nose, but with the **Neutral Mask**. This was a simple, featureless leather mask with a calm, neutral expression. The purpose of the mask was to erase the student's own facial tics, habits, and psychological mannerisms. By neutralizing their faces, the student was forced to discover a new economy and power in their physical body. They had to learn to communicate through gestures, posture, and breath alone. It was a process of unlearning, of stripping away the social and personal "noise" to find a state of pure physical presence. A student wearing the Neutral Mask was expected to move with a sense of calm, balance, and readiness, like a cat poised to pounce. This state of neutrality, which Lecoq called *disponibilité*, was the essential foundation upon which all other characters, including the clown, would be built.

Only after mastering this state of neutrality were students introduced to the world of the clown. The key to this discovery was the smallest mask in the world: the **red nose**. For Lecoq, the red nose was a powerful tool of revelation. The moment a student put on the nose, they were entering a different state of being. The rules of normal human interaction no longer apply. They were given permission to be stupid, to be vulnerable, and to fail. Lecoq's method was famously about finding one's personal clown, or, more accurately, allowing it to emerge. He believed that everyone has a clown inside them, and that this inner clown is intimately linked to their own unique physique, personality, and, most importantly, their personal failings.

The training involved a series of improvisations and exercises designed to push the student into a state where their intellectual defenses would crumble. Lecoq would encourage his students to find their personal **"flop"** (*bide*), that specific area of life where they are most beautifully incompetent. One person's clown might be defined by their complete inability to handle a simple prop; another might be their pathetic attempts at being seductive; a third's might be their over-the-top displays of emotion. The goal was not to hide this failure, but to embrace it, amplify it, and celebrate it. The Lecoq clown finds immense joy in his own magnificent ineptitude. When a trick goes wrong, he does not get frustrated; he is delighted by the surprise of his own failure. It is this resilience, this ability to find pleasure in the flop, that creates the deep connection with the audience. We see our own vulnerabilities reflected in the clown's failures, and we are moved and amused by his refusal to be defeated by them.

The result of this training was not a troupe of identical

performers, but a collection of unique and deeply personal clowns. Lecoq was not teaching his students *how* to be funny; he was creating the conditions for them to discover *their own* unique funniness. His legacy is a poetic and profound one. He reconnected the clown to the art of the actor and the poet, proving that the red nose could be a key to unlocking not just broad comedy, but the deepest truths of the human condition.

The Tyranny of Fun: The Gaulier Philosophy and "Le Jeu"

If Jacques Lecoq was the calm, analytical architect of the modern clown, Philippe Gaulier is his provocative, chaotic, and often infuriating counterpart. A former student and teacher at Lecoq's school, Gaulier broke away to found his own institution, the École Philippe Gaulier, where he cultivated a philosophy that was both a continuation of and a rebellion against his mentor's methods. For Gaulier, the key to clowning is not found in neutrality or the analysis of failure, but in the relentless pursuit of pleasure and "le jeu"the game. His teaching style is legendary for its brutal honesty and its unwavering focus on the joy of performance.

At the heart of Gaulier's philosophy is the idea that the clown is a beautiful idiot who finds an ecstatic pleasure in their own stupidity and in their complicity with the audience. The primary job of the clown is to have fun, and to make sure the audience can see that they are having fun. This sounds simple, but in Gaulier's classroom, it is a formidable challenge. He is notorious for his confrontational approach. As his students perform, he sits on the sidelines, acting as a ruthless barometer of their success. If a student is boring, if they are "hiding" behind a clever idea, or if they are not genuinely in a state of play, Gaulier will stop them, often with a loud and dismissive critique. His goal is to strip away the performer's intellectual ego, to force them to abandon their carefully constructed plans and simply exist in a state of joyful, idiotic presence.

Unlike Lecoq, Gaulier is less interested in the "why" of failure and more interested in the "pleasure" of it. A Gaulier-trained clown does not just accept their flop; they revel in it. They find their mistakes to be the most wonderful and amusing things in the world. This creates a powerful connection with the audience, who become co-conspirators in the clown's delight. Gaulier teaches that the audience is everything. A clown must be constantly looking at the audience, checking in, sharing the pleasure of their own idiocy. "The clown," he famously says, "is a red nose, a costume, and one thousand complicit eyes." This relationship is paramount. Without the audience's laughter and complicity, the clown does not exist.

The Gaulier classroom is a place of high stakes and often high emotions. Students are pushed to their limits, forced to confront their fears of judgment and their need to be clever. The process can be grueling, but the goal is liberation. Gaulier seeks to free the performer from the tyranny of their own intelligence, to help them find a state of beautiful, uninhibited foolishness where they are no longer performing *for* the audience but playing *with* them. The successful Gaulier clown is not pathetic; they are triumphant in their stupidity. They are a radiant beacon of pleasure, and the laughter they generate is not one of pity or superiority, but one of shared, infectious joy. His graduates, which include celebrated performers like Sacha Baron Cohen and Emma Thompson, are known for their fearless, provocative, and intensely playful approach to comedy, a testament to a teaching style that finds truth not in quiet analysis, but in a loud, joyful, and relentless game.

The All-American Big Top: The Ringling Bros. Clown College

While the Parisian schools were developing a theatrical and philosophical approach to clowning, a very different and equally influential institution was taking shape in America. This was the Ringling Bros. and Barnum & Bailey Clown College, an institution that was, for decades, the single most important training ground for circus clowns in the world. Founded in 1968, Clown College was not an intellectual acting conservatory; it was a pragmatic, highly specialized trade school. Its mission was not to help performers find their inner fool, but to produce professional, entertaining clowns who could fill a role in "The Greatest Show on Earth."

The curriculum at Clown College was a whirlwind of practical skills. The philosophy was that a good circus clown had to be a jack-of-all-trades. Students were given intensive training in a vast array of disciplines. They learned the fundamentals of slapsticks, including how to take a convincing pratfall without injury. They studied juggling, unicycling, stilt-walking, and basic acrobatics. They were taught the art of mime and pantomime, learning how to tell a story with their bodies in a way that could be understood from the furthest reaches of a three-ring circus arena. They also learned the essential, practical arts of the trade: how to design and apply their unique makeup, how to construct and repair their own props, and how to build a "gag" from the ground up.

Unlike the European schools that emphasized the discovery of a personal clown, Clown College operated on the American circus tradition of archetypes. Students were taught the history and function of the Whiteface, the Auguste, and the Tramp. While they were encouraged to develop a unique persona within these frameworks, the primary goal was to create a character that would fit into the larger ecosystem of the Ringling Bros. Clown Alley. The emphasis was on clarity, readability, and effectiveness. A gag had to "read" to an audience of thousands, so the comedy had to be big, broad, and instantly understandable.

The audition process was famously competitive, and the training was intense. An eight-to-ten-week program would cram years of circus knowledge into a grueling schedule. The faculty was composed of veteran circus clowns, masters of the craft like Lou Jacobs and Frosty Little, who passed down the gags and traditions that had been honed over a century of performance. The final exam was an audition for the circus itself. A graduating class might see only a handful of its members offer a coveted contract to tour with the show.

Clown College was a profoundly American institution. It was practical, results-oriented, and deeply connected to the commercial realities of the entertainment business. It created a standardized, high-quality product: the Ringling clown, a performer equipped with a wide range of skills and a deep understanding of what it took to make a massive, diverse audience laugh. While it was criticized by some for being a "clown factory" that stifled the more personal, poetic aspects of the art form, its influence is undeniable. For over three decades, it was the premier gateway to a professional career in American circus clowning. It preserved and passed on a century of circus knowledge, and its graduates populated the clown alleys of nearly every major circus in the country, ensuring that the classic archetypes and timeless gags of the American big top would continue to entertain new generations of families.

CHAPTER TEN

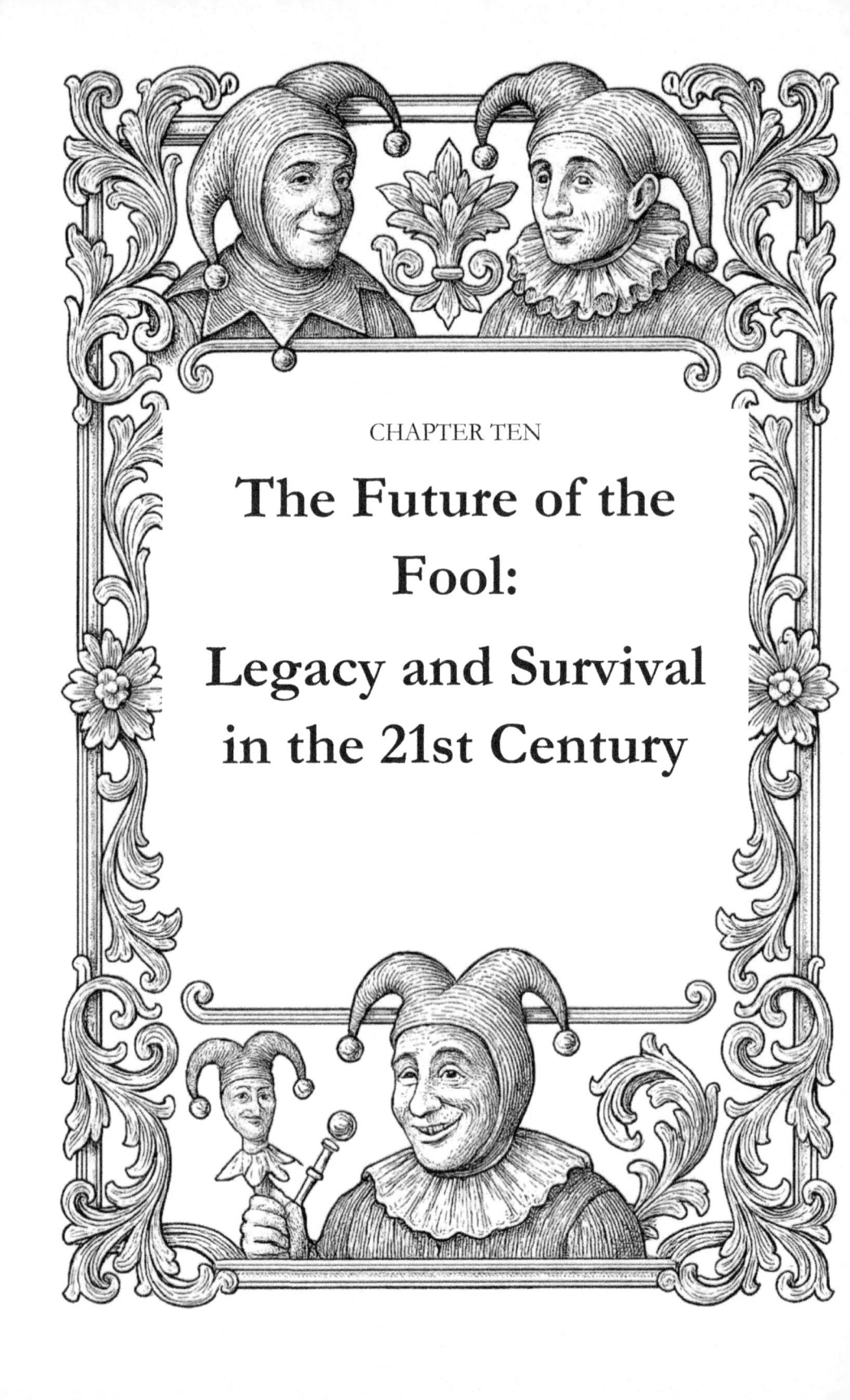

The Future of the Fool:

Legacy and Survival in the 21st Century

The story of the clown is a long and winding road, a journey that has taken the fool from the sun-drenched steps of ancient temples to the muddy fields of medieval fairs, from the gilded halls of royal courts to the vast, noisy expanse of the three-ring circus. We have followed him as he transformed from a sacred shaman into a political satirist, from a tragic poet into a television pitchman. We have seen his painted smile evolve from a mask of divine otherness to a symbol of childhood joy, and we have witnessed that same smile curdles into a rictus of pure terror. The clown has been celebrated, feared, psychoanalyzed, deconstructed, and reborn, time and time again. He is perhaps the most resilient and adaptable archetype in human culture, a character who has survived the fall of empires, the birth of new technologies, and the seismic shifts of social change.

Now, as we stand in the early decades of the 21st century, the fool finds himself at another crossroads. The traditional stages that defined him for generations—the travelling circus, the variety show, the local television program—are either gone or fading into memory. He lives in a world that is more connected and yet more fractured than ever before, a digital landscape of viral memes, online tribes, and fleeting attention spans. The clown's legacy is a deeply fractured one, his identity split between the benevolent healer and the malevolent monster. The central question, then, is what becomes of him now? In a world of artificial intelligence, virtual reality, and profound global anxiety, what is the role of the fool? This final chapter will assess the clown's current, paradoxical state and speculate on his future, asking the ultimate question: in the world of tomorrow, will we still need a clown to show us what it means to be human today?

The Inherited Duality: A Culture of Laughter and Fear

The modern clown does not exist as a single, coherent entity; he is a walking, honking contradiction. He lives in a state of profound cultural schizophrenia, simultaneously occupying two extreme and opposing poles in our collective imagination. At one end of the spectrum is the clown as a therapeutic agent, a healer whose primary tool is laughter. At the other end is the clown as a malevolent predator, a figure of pure dread. The 21st-century fool is defined by this duality, and our cultural landscape is a testament to the fact that we have learned to hold both of these conflicting ideas in our heads at the same time.

The image of the healing clown has its most powerful modern avatar in the work of humanitarian organizations like **Clowns Without Borders** and in the philosophy of medical pioneers like **Patch Adams**. This movement represents a return to the clown's most ancient and sacred function: to provide psychological and spiritual relief in times of crisis. These therapeutic clowns, who enter refugee camps, disaster zones, and sterile hospital wards, are not simply entertainers. They are practitioners of what can only be described as emotional first aid. They use the universal language of play and laughter to reintroduce a sense of normalcy, safety, and hope into environments defined by trauma and fear. Their work is a powerful testament to the idea that laughter is not a luxury, but a fundamental human need, a psychological survival mechanism. In a world wracked by conflict and crisis, this vision of the clown as a selfless, benevolent healer is more relevant and necessary than ever. It is the fool in his purest form, absorbing the world's suffering and transforming it into shared joy.

Yet, for every heartwarming image of a clown making a refugee child laugh, there is a chilling image of **Pennywise** lurking in a storm drain. The "evil clown," a trope that was supercharged in the late 20th century, has become a permanent and dominant fixture in our culture. The character of **The Joker**, once a campy prankster, is now routinely reimagined as a terrifying agent of nihilistic chaos, earning actors Academy Awards for his portrayal. The horror genre continues to mine coulrophobia for profit, churning out films and television shows that rely on the jump-scare power of a sinister, painted face. The clown has become a reliable monster, a convenient shorthand for the concept of corrupted innocence.

The coexistence of these two extremes, the healer and the monster, is one of the defining features of the clown's modern identity. He has become a cultural Rorschach test. Our individual reaction to the image of a clown often reveals more about our own psychological landscape than it does about the character himself. Do we see a figure of fun and empathy, or a symbol of deception and threat? The clown has become a mirror reflecting our own hopes and fears about the world. He contains multitudes because *we* contain multitudes. We live in an age of great anxiety, but also one of great compassion. The modern clown, in his fractured and contradictory state, is simply holding up a mirror to the profound duality of our times. He is both our best hope and our worst fear, a perfect fool for an age of extremes.

The Shrinking Circus and the Search for a New Stage

For over a century, the spiritual and professional home of the clown was the circus. The big top was his cathedral, the sawdust rings his altar. It was here that the great American archetypes were born and refined, and it was here that generations of families had their most memorable encounters with the fool. The closure of the Ringling Bros. and Barnum & Bailey Circus in 2017 was therefore more than just the end of a business; it was a seismic event in the history of the clown. It signaled the end of an era and raised a crucial question: if the big top is gone, where does the clown go now?

The decline of the traditional traveling circus was the result of a perfect storm of factors. Animal rights concerns made the use of elephants and other exotic animals increasingly untenable. The rise of sophisticated, on-demand digital entertainment made the comparatively simple spectacle of the circus seem quaint and old-fashioned. The business model, which required a massive logistical operation to move a city-sized show from town to town, became financially unsustainable. With the closure of its flagship institution also came the closure of the **Ringling Bros. Clown College**, the single most important pipeline for professional circus clowns in America for over three decades. An entire ecosystem that had supported and defined the American clown for a century had vanished.

However, the death of the big top did not mean the death of the circus clown; it meant the beginning of an evolution. The clown, true to his resilient nature, began to search for new stages. This has led to a flourishing of smaller, more innovative, and often more adult-oriented forms of circus. Companies like **Cirque du Soleil** reimagined the circus as a theatrical spectacle, weaving acrobatics, music, and clowning into a coherent narrative. The clowns in these shows are rarely the bumbling interrupters of the old three-ring format; they are often central characters, silent poets, or mythic guides who drive the story forward. Their comedy is more integrated, more subtle, and often more poignant.

Beyond these new theatrical circuses, individual clowns have become entrepreneurial nomads, adapting their skills to a wide variety of new venues. The classic Auguste or Tramp, once confined to the circus ring, can now be found performing at corporate events, trade shows, Renaissance fairs, and community festivals. They have become freelance agents of joy, bringing their highly specialized skills to audiences in a piecemeal fashion. While this provides a living, it represents a fundamental shift in the clown's status. He is no longer the star of a massive spectacle, but a niche entertainer, a curious novelty in a crowded entertainment marketplace. His stage has shrunk, but in doing so, it has also diversified, forcing him to be more adaptable and resourceful than ever before.

The Digital Fool: Beyond Memes and Panics

As the physical stages for clowning were shrinking, a vast and chaotic new stage was opening: the internet. Initially, as we have seen, the internet seemed hostile to the clown, reducing him to a creepy meme or a viral threat. However, as digital platforms have matured, a new generation of performers has begun to skillfully harness their power, proving that the ancient art of the fool can thrive in the age of the algorithm.

Platforms like **TikTok**, with its emphasis on short-form video, have become a natural home for a new kind of clowning. The format is perfectly suited for the quick, visual gag—the modern equivalent of a classic circus "walkaround." A new wave of performers, many of them trained in the theatrical traditions of Lecoq and Gaulier, are using these platforms to build massive followings. They create short, silent films, perform absurd character-based sketches, and engage in a form of digital slapstick that is perfectly calibrated for a mobile audience with a short attention span. This digital stage offers an unprecedented of creative freedom. A clown no longer needs to be hired by a circus or a television network to find an audience. They can build their own "ring" on their smartphone, developing a direct and intimate relationship with their followers.

This new digital clown is a hybrid creature. They combine the classic physical comedy of the silent film era with the self-aware, often surreal humor of the internet. They can be poignant and pathetic one moment, and absurdly chaotic the next. They are masters of a new kind of performance, one that blurs the line between the scripted gag and the seemingly spontaneous, "authentic" moment. This digital renaissance is allowing the clown to bypass the traditional gatekeepers and reconnect directly with the public, proving that the demand for well-crafted, intelligent foolishness is still immense.

However, this new stage comes with its own set of challenges. The internet thrives on novelty, and the pressure to create a constant stream of new content can be creatively exhausting. The algorithm, not a ringmaster, dictates what is seen, and online fame can be notoriously fickle. Furthermore, while a clown can gain millions of followers, monetizing that fame—turning "likes" into a sustainable living—remains a difficult proposition. The digital fool must be not only a brilliant performer but also a savvy social media strategist, a brand manager, and a content creator. It is a new and demanding set of skills, but for those who can master it, the internet offers a global stage of unimaginable size, a place where a single, perfect pratfall can be seen by more people in an hour than would have seen a classic circus clown in a lifetime.

The Enduring Need for the Fool

So what is the future of this ancient, adaptable, and profound human archetype? The clown will undoubtedly continue to evolve. We may one day see clowns in **virtual reality**, creating interactive, immersive worlds of play where the audience is not just a spectator but a direct participant in the sublime stupidity. We may see **artificial intelligence** used to generate scripts or assist in the creation of gags, though it is hard to imagine a machine ever replicating the essential, vulnerable humanity of a great clown's "flop."

The stages will change, the makeup will be reinvented, and the gags will be adapted for new technologies, but the clown's fundamental purpose will remain. The core functions of the fool—to speak truth to power, to heal through laughter, to hold a mirror to society's follies, and to celebrate our shared, imperfect humanity—are not relics of a bygone era. They are, if anything, more necessary now than ever before. In a world that often feels dangerously polarized and relentlessly serious, we need the jester to puncture our self-importance. In an age of anxiety and trauma, we need the therapeutic clown to remind us of the healing power of joy. And in a culture that is increasingly curated, filtered, and virtually simulated, we need the fool to show us what is gloriously, beautifully, and hilariously real.

The clown will survive because he represents an essential part of ourselves. He is our capacity for resilience, our ability to fall and get back up again, to face the absurdity of the world with a honk and a smile. He is the embodiment of our own magnificent failures and the triumphant spirit that allows us to find joy in them. The costumes will change, the platforms will evolve, but the human need for a figure who can absorb our fears, mock our pretensions, and lead us in the revolutionary act of laughter is eternal. The future of the fool is secure, because the future, like the past, will always need him.

For Further Reading

The story of the clown is as vast as it is colorful. For those whose curiosity has been sparked, the resources listed below offer a deeper dive into the rich history and complex psychology of this enduring archetype. Whether you are a student of theatre, a history enthusiast, or simply a curious reader, these books, documentaries, and organizations provide an excellent starting point for further exploration.

Books

- **Towsen, John H.** *Clowns.* **Hawthorn Books, 1976.** An essential and comprehensive historical overview of the clown, from ancient archetypes to the 20th-century circus. A foundational text for any student of the subject.
- **Stott, Andrew McConnell.** *The Pantomime Life of*

Joseph Grimaldi: Laughter, Madness and the Story of Britain's Greatest Comedian. **Canongate Books, 2009.** A brilliant biography of the man who invented the modern clown, painting a vivid picture of Georgian London and the brutal physicality of early stage performance.
- **Lecoq, Jacques.** *The Moving Body: Teaching Creative Theatre*. **Methuen Drama, 2002.** The seminal text from the master teacher himself, outlining his philosophy on physical theatre, neutrality, and the discovery of the personal clown. Essential reading for understanding the modern theatrical fool.
- **Radin, Paul.** *The Trickster: A Study in American Indian Mythology*. **Schocken, 1972.** A classic anthropological study that explores the role of the trickster and sacred clown figure in Native American cultures, providing a crucial non-European perspective.
- **Carlyon, David.** *Dan Rice: The Most Famous Man You've Never Heard Of*. **PublicAffairs, 2001.** A fascinating look at one of America's most important 19th-century circus clowns, whose humor was deeply political and satirical.

Documentaries

- *The Circus***. Directed by Sharon Grimberg, American Experience / PBS, 2018.** A sweeping and beautifully produced documentary series that covers the rise and fall of the American traveling circus, with significant attention paid to the evolution of its iconic clowns.
- *Wrinkles the Clown***. Directed by Michael Beach Nichols, 2019.** A captivating and unsettling look at the "creepy clown" phenomenon, focusing on a real-life

viral figure in Florida. It serves as an excellent case study on coulrophobia and internet folklore.
- *The American Meme***. Directed by Bert Marcus, 2018.** While not about clowns specifically, this documentary provides crucial insight into the world of digital fame and the lives of online personalities, a relevant context for understanding the "digital fool."

Organizations and Resources

- **Clowns Without Borders International:** The official resource for information on the work of therapeutic clowns operating in conflict zones and crisis areas around the world. Their website provides reports, photos, and information on their ongoing projects.
- **The Circus Historical Society:** An organization dedicated to preserving the history of the circus, particularly in America. Their publications and archives are an invaluable resource for information on famous performers, shows, and traditions.
- **École Philippe Gaulier** and **École Internationale de Théâtre Jacques Lecoq:** The websites for these two premier French theatre schools offer insight into their distinct philosophies and the modern art of clown training.

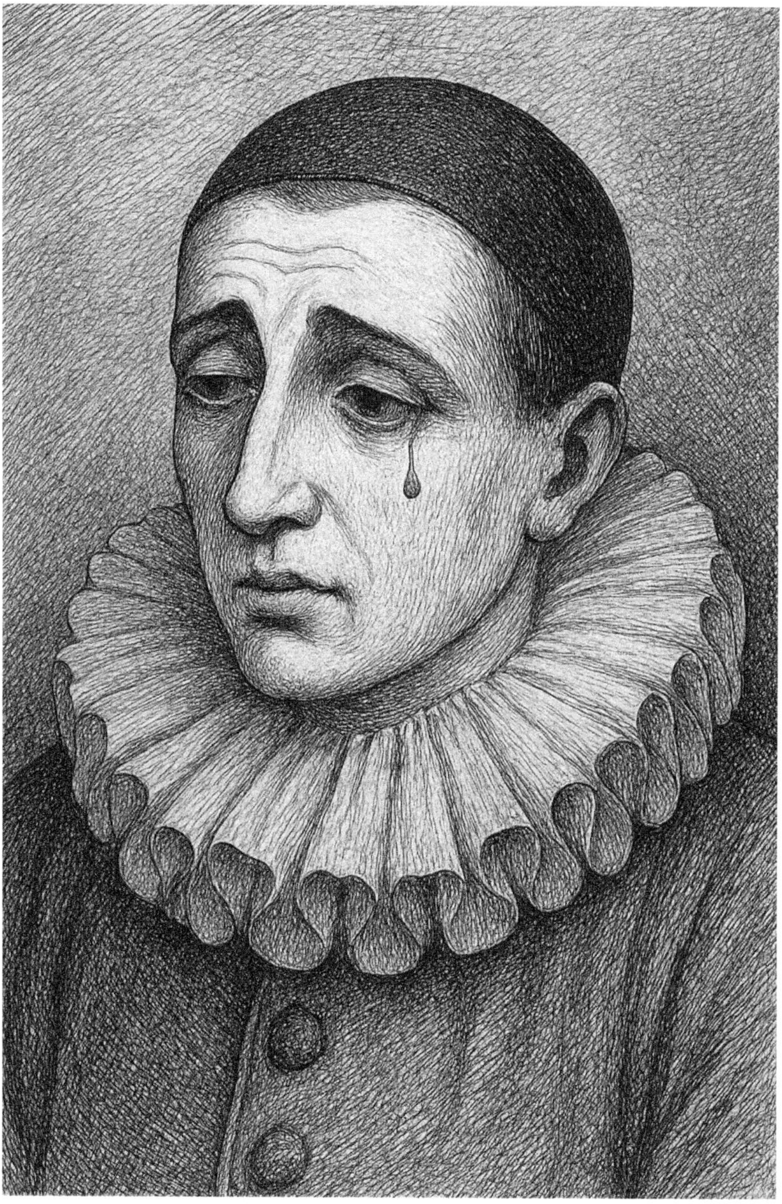

Printed in Dunstable, United Kingdom